The Time is Now

Mandate, Ministry and Mantle

By Bishop Jeff Coleman

GUIDED PATH
PUBLISHING

ISBN 979-8-9869918-7-0 (eBook)

ISBN 979-8-9869918-6-3 (Print)

CONTENTS

THE TIME IS NOW

When complacency exceeds the desire for change, the consequence is concession and chaos. But when comfort and contentment no longer pacify the people, the cry freedom at any cost can be heard, and it alone becomes the catalyst for confrontation and change. Unfortunately, the body of Christ has seldom been prepared for tremendous opportunities that God has provided through history. At the end of WWII, General Douglas MacArthur appealed to American churches, saying of Japan, "Send me 10,000 missionaries and I will give you a Christian nation." The response was tepid at best. When the Berlin Wall fell and communism cracked under the weight of its own corruption, a few intrepid organizations seized the opportunity for the growth of Christianity in regions where it had been unknown, but by and large the church missed an advantageous opening for evangelization.

In many cases, the difference between success and failure is the ability to recognize certain moments that only God

Himself can provide. This is as true for individuals as it is for organizations. In his book *The Time is Now*, my friend, City Harvest Network Bishop Jeff Coleman, points out the importance of not only recognizing, but accessing open doors that lead to personal growth, evangelizing your world, and fulfilling all the purposes for which God called you into His kingdom. His message is clear: you don't have to be satisfied with what is mundane and mediocre. You can boldly step forward into a future that pleases heaven and horrifies hell—and you can do it now. God has planned a strategic path before you, and He is beckoning you to forget the failures of your past and embark on a journey that becomes sweeter and more satisfying every day.

Dr. Rod Parsley
Pastor and Founder, World Harvest Church
Columbus, Ohio

"Freedom is never more than one generation away from extinction. We didn't pass it to our children in the bloodstream. It must be fought for protected, and handed on for them to do the same."

— PRESIDENT RONALD REAGAN

CHAPTER 1

THE TIME IS NOW

This is War! There is a battle that is already raging for our own lives, as well as for our families, our nation, and our world. With all of the chaos going on, the world is trying to silence the church, screaming that we are outdated or out of touch with the present. Comparing our culture to that of sixty years ago, or even back in Biblical times, we know from scripture that the battles we face are very similar to those in history. There are many parallels between the nations Paul referenced in his writing and what we see today. Our God is the same yesterday, today, and forever and His word remains true and completely relevant to come against the war that we find ourselves up against today. More than anything, God is a God of love and desires to have a relationship with His people. I want to give you the foundation to stand and fight as a believer, strengthen your relationship with Him, and help us reclaim the forward momentum of the Great Commission.

As Christians, we must resist the paradigm shift that characterizes American life in the twenty-first century. Our culture encourages working long hours to make as much money as possible and maxing out credit cards, piling up debt to buy the fanciest cars, homes, and toys. There can be pressure to "Keep up with the Joneses." For many, the church is a weekly obligation to "fit in if possible," with churches offering several different service options to accommodate your weekly schedule. Churches have also avoided the confrontation of sin entering the church, based on the fear that it would affect their numbers, reputation, or collection plate. If this cultural shift was a positive one, our world would appear to be a very different place. Gallup polls currently cite climbing statistics of depression and debt, while numbers of churchgoers and Biblical literacy are plummeting. God has become an afterthought for many, and the concept of a "relationship" has been lost. We cannot continue to look in the other direction and allow so many people to live without the revelation of who God is.

So, let me make this clear: I am not blaming the world for its condition. In essence, the world is unaware that they are missing the mark. The church's role is to bring truth, revelation, healing, and salvation to a lost and dying world around us. This book is a clarion call to the Body of Christ to awaken, rise, and touch the world around it! The Time is Now, and you were created for this time. In these next chapters, you will be challenged to realize your destiny in Christ and place your name among the pillars of the faith as a true world changer! Just as Ronald Reagan said, freedom is something that we must fight for. We must fight for our children to have the freedom to worship in this country, just as we can today. Looking around us, we can see that the freedom to worship the one true God is currently under attack.

We must fight to defend our children, ensuring the "correct" truth is passed on to them. Merely watching the news briefly can leave people questioning where God is or what is happening to our world. Many parents are nervous about sending their children to school due to safety risks and concern about what their children are being taught! America's moral fiber is being stretched to its core. Meanwhile, Christians are safely tucked behind the walls of our churches, singing "Onward Christian Soldier." We must take up our cross and head toward the frontline, facing the outright attack on America. It's a call to city council meetings, school board meetings, voter booths, and city streets. We have a responsibility to be the light to the world, even in our community. For too long, Christians have been content fading to the background, and that is not where God called us to stand!

Churches must come out from behind the pews before we are blotted out from the pages of history. You could say that this is a war on all fronts; however, I want to encourage you that when we as Christians become strengthened in who we are in Him and walk as a body toward a common goal, we will have victory! This book is a call from the pages of the scripture to discover and walk in the calling God has for your life, to believe for His promises to come to pass in your life, and to open your eyes to the miraculous work He is doing around you! It is easy to sit back and think that you can start tomorrow, but I implore you: the time is now!

TIME TO REBUILD

Here's the thing, you may be reading this thinking that you aren't ready to step in to fight against all of the chaos that is going on in the world. You read the headlines or watch the videos on your newsfeed, and it makes you sick to your stomach. I imagine thoughts like, "But there are people out there who can handle that. There are people who are called to step in and fight to turn the world back around. Some pastors and evangelists and prophets can speak up for the church!" While these and the other members of the Five Fold Ministry have a job to do, these responsibilities do not rest solely on their shoulders. You actually have a ministry in your backyard! The task of going out into the world to advocate, pray, and stand in the gap for the unsaved people in our world is up to all believers. I challenge believers to step out of the shadows so that we might find unity to turn our society back to our savior!

In the beginning of the book of Nehemiah, he received troubling news about the state of the province of Judah. The Jews who had returned from captivity were in danger, and the wall of Jerusalem had been torn down. In Nehemiah 1:4-7, the Message Bible says, "When I heard this, I sat down and wept. I mourned for days, fasting and praying before the God of Heaven. I said, 'God, God of Heaven, the great and awesome God, loyal to his covenant and faithful to those who love him and obey his commands: Look at me, listen to me. Pay attention to this prayer of your servant. I'm praying day and night in intercession for your servants, the People of Israel, confessing their sins. And I'm including myself, I and my ancestors, among those who have sinned against you.

We've treated you like dirt: We haven't done what you told us, haven't followed your commands, and haven't respected the decisions you gave to Moses, your servant."

Later in Nehemiah, he led them, as the Jews had the seemingly impossible task of rebuilding the walls of Jerusalem, even under the scrutiny and threat of an attack. Nehemiah 4:11 (MSG) says, "And all this time, our enemies were saying, 'They won't know what hit them. Before they know it, we'll be at their throats, killing them right and left. That will put a stop to the work!" Instead of bowing and surrendering, Nehemiah persevered. In verses 13-14, scripture says, "So I stationed armed guards at the most vulnerable places of the wall and assigned people by families with their swords, lances, and bows. After looking things over, I stood up and spoke to the nobles, officials, and everyone else: 'Don't be afraid of them. Put your minds on the Master great and awesome, and then fight for your brothers, sons, daughters, wives, and homes.'" You are where you are, living when you're living for a reason. He has given you the gifts and talents you possess because He has the big picture of who you are. Practice declaring who you are in Him to become confident in holding the tools he's handed you.

The truth is that you can help shift our society back toward worshipping the one true God! You have a calling in your life. God created you with a purpose, and it is a purpose that only you can accomplish! God is calling you to take your place to fight, but first and foremost, He is calling you to develop your personal relationship with Him as Lord and Savior of your life. As you grow in your relationship with Him, setting the example in your home and interceding for your family, He will start to reveal to you the plan that He has for you: the mantle you will carry and the ministry you will walk in, to ensure that our future generations will continue to walk in freedom.

ROMANS 13:11-14 (MSG)

But make sure you don't get so absorbed and exhausted in taking care of all your day-by-day obligations that you lose track of time and doze off, oblivious to God. The night is about over, and dawn is about to break. Be up and awake to what God is doing! God is putting the finishing touches on the salvation work he began when we first believed. We can't afford to waste a minute, must not squander these precious daylight hours in frivolity and indulgence, in sleeping around and dissipation, in bickering and grabbing everything in sight. Get out of bed and get dressed! Don't loiter and linger, waiting until the very last minute. Dress yourselves in Christ, and be up and about!

DO IT TODAY

Several years ago, I witnessed firsthand how quickly life can change. We were at the end of a church service, and I followed the prompting of the Holy Spirit to offer an altar call for people to receive Jesus as their savior. A woman came up with her young children clinging onto her. She told me she wanted to be saved, so I led her in the prayer for salvation. I received word that within less than a week, that woman passed away in her sleep. I imagine there had been people praying for her to be saved. There were probably people who planted seeds, telling her about Jesus, maybe offering prayer for healing, and inviting her to church. If those pieces had not happened, if I had not heeded the prompting from the Holy Spirit, or if she had not accepted the urge to respond, her eternity would be very different. From Romans 13:11-14, I urge you not to wait until the last minute; this is important! Don't wait until the last minute to get your relationship with Christ back on track. Don't postpone reaching out to your family; when you feel the nudge to pray for your coworker, respond immediately! When that woman was tucking her children into bed that evening, she had plans for the next day, week, month, and years. I am so thankful that she made the choice that day for Jesus.

To take part in salvation, just like previously mentioned, is something that every follower of Christ is called to. As you deepen your relationship with Christ, becoming more familiar with the leading of the Holy Spirit, you will be able to follow after the unction and be the hands and feet of Christ. Sometimes, it will be instrumental in transforming someone's life, or it could contribute to a promise you believe in His Word. You may never even see the results of your act of obedience to His leading. His plan and reasons for leading us to do these tasks are above our understanding. Differing from how our society views Christianity and attending church, we are called to be the church. John 14:11-14 in the Message Bible says, "Believe me: I am in my Father, and my Father is in me. If you don't believe that, then believe what you see: these works. The person who trusts me will not only do what I'm doing but even greater things, because I, on my way to the Father, am giving you the same work to do that I've been doing. You can count on it. From now on, whatever you request along the lines of who I am and what I am doing, I'll do it. That's how the Father will be seen for who he is in the Son. I mean it. Whatever you request in this way, I'll do." We can trust that God is faithful to fulfill the promises in His Word. As we obey His direction, He can use us to speak into the lives of people around us. He can also lead us to the open door for the promises we believe to come to pass.

PURPOSE IN EVERYTHING

I believe that the time we are walking into will be remarkable when we will see His answers happening more quickly than we could imagine. They could take place faster than time would typically allow! I call these quick, immediate miracles, God's "suddenlies." We will see God move in ways that defy time, or at least our current understanding of time! This is the time to possess the open doors of your future! How God is preparing you, as well as His ability to perform miracles outside of time, will result in miracles coming to pass in your life. You have to let go of your past to lay hold of your future. You may have walked through painful situations or a traumatic childhood or be carrying wounds from the past that make it difficult to continue to believe that God is a faithful God who answers prayer. You may not have been in a relationship with Christ for very long and have yet to see His movement firsthand! You have to let go of the disappointment of your delayed dreams. You must begin to hope and trust again. God is good, and you can believe that! You must be willing to act, to say "NO!" to the devil's lies, and to say a "YES!" to the promises of God! So don't give up on your dreams!

We can read about several faith leaders, both men and

women, who clung to their beliefs even when they seemed impossible. There is always a purpose in the preparation. If you think of preparation as the action or process of making something ready, we can see that God has a purpose in the preparation! Consider the example of the lives of Joseph, Moses, and Esther. God was preparing Joseph for the various stages of his life, going from home to slave and from prison to being with Pharaoh.

Regarding Moses, most of his life was spent in stages and phases of preparation! God trained Moses for several situations he would encounter while leading the Israelites. Esther was instrumental in advocating for her people. She stepped up, even when it could have led to her death.

When God combines preparation with His miraculous handling of time, it can change the atmosphere. It can turn the outcome, bringing glory to His name! The results are seen in the situations where the "suddenlies" come to pass! When the breakthrough comes, it erases the weariness of the previous season, a refreshing presence of the Lord comes upon you, and you know that the waiting was worth the outcome. As the reader, I want to encourage you to take hold of the preparation. We can learn through the word; understanding the pillars that stabilize the believer's life. Through this support and strengthening, you can be used more effectively and confidently in the ministry that God is calling you to, carrying the mantle that only you can sustain and taking your specific place to rebuild the wall. As the body of Christ, this is a reminder of the responsibility that we carry in our world. I believe that we will soon start to see a shift occur. We can start gaining the ground we have lost and reclaim it for Christ!

"I know you are about to rise and show your tender love to Zion. Now is the time, Lord, for your compassion and mercy to be poured out. The appointed time has come for your prophetic promises to be fulfilled."

— PSALMS 102:13 TPT

CHAPTER 2

CHRONOS/KAIROS

God desires to take you to higher and greater levels. There are promises you believe in, and I truly believe that now is the time to see God working in your life! He has plans for you that will happen in a shorter time than you expect! God will reveal himself as the God of time and distance in your life. Scripture provides us with countless miracles of God moving outside our time "concept." Rather than the devil always being to blame, time (or our perception of time) and flesh have stopped countless moves of God. The ancient Greeks had two words for time and how time is measured: Kairos and Chronos. Understanding the two very different meanings of time is vital to both your understanding of the miraculous works of Christ and the capacity to believe for something to occur outside of the constraints of chronological time.

CHRONOS VS. KAIROS

Chronos is a quantitative word, referring to time we can measure in seconds, minutes, hours, and days. This is the time we attempt to measure numerically. It is where the English language gets the word "chronological," and we keep track of this time on calendars. We have been bound in a place where we live daily, minute to minute, second to second, waiting to see what will happen. Chronos time has also imposed limits on what could "possibly" happen. For example, an earthly harvest: if you miss planting your seed in the fall, you must wait all year for fall to return. On a personal level, you may think you're too old; you can believe you've gone too far, or you assume you'll never be able to get "there." Sometimes, you can be convinced that you have completely missed your opportunity. Those mindsets are all translated from thinking in linear time—Chronos time.

Kairos refers to the quality. This ancient Greek word can mean opportunity, season, or fitting time. Kairos refers to time that is not operating on the calendar and is outside of living hour to hour. A Kairos moment is when the Holy Spirit is moving and ready to act. It is an invitation to cooperate with the Holy Spirit at that very moment. God wants to give us Kairos moments where we are ready to be involved in His move on the earth. God already set his calendar, and it's completely outside of our time constraints.

"I know you are about to rise and show your tender love to Zion. Now is the time, Lord, for your compassion and mercy to be poured out. The appointed time has come for your prophetic promises to be fulfilled." Psalms 102:13 TPT. To be a part of His Kairos moments, we must transition to a mindset that the set time on God's calendar of eternity will no longer be counted in seconds, hours, days, or months. God has been showing me that I must live this year in moments. I will tell you right now you are a moment waiting to happen. You're about to step right into the middle of your miracle. You're about to show right up in the middle of a situation. You're about to walk into a room and be on God's time clock as soon as you enter that place. God said, now is the time, Kairos time. The time is now! We must seek God for the Kairos moments in our lives and be ready to be a part of His work on earth.

KAIROS MIRACLES

The Bible reveals only a portion of the miracles since Genesis. Many of those miracles demonstrated instances of God working through Kairos' time, disregarding our understanding of Chronos' time. Ephesians 5:1 tells us we are to be followers of God as dear children. The Amplified Bible reveals that we should "be imitators of God [copy Him and follow His example], as well-beloved children imitate their father." When God created the universe, He spoke words of faith and life: "LIGHT BE!" And light obeyed! You and I are to speak just like Him. God gives us clear instructions that we may be key participants in the work He desires to do. We must follow His word and His voice. Jesus explains in John 5:19 that He follows His Father's example to know what to do and speak. We must be imitators of Christ, following His example and seeking Him for instructions so that we may do the greater works now, as He commands.

In Joshua 6, it tells us that God has given the city of Jericho to Joshua; however, this passage also gives very specific instructions on seeing this promise come to fruition. Joshua and his people were to march around the city once a day for six days. On the seventh day, they were to march around the city seven times, and priests were to blow the horns. When the priests blew one long blast on the ram's horn, all the people were to shout as loud as they could. In verse 10: "But Joshua commanded the people, saying 'You shall not shout nor let your voice be heard, nor let a word proceed from your mouth until the day I tell you, 'Shout!' Then you shall shout!'" In Verse 20: "So the people shouted, and the priests blew the trumpets; and when the people heard the sound of the trumpet, the people shouted with a great shout, and the wall fell flat, so that the people went up into the city, everyone straight ahead, and they took the city." (NASB 2020)

The structure and organization of this city demonstrate that it was only through a miraculous work of God that the wall fell, and they were able to obtain victory. He told them to labor for six days by walking. And as they walked, they were to keep their mouths shut. This was a time of transition from a place of what they could do to a place where they were to praise Him for what only He could do. Praise is expectation. I don't praise Him because of my situation. I praise Him because of my revelation. Your reflection of the goodness of God can lead you to a place where time collapses. That seed would have taken a long time, more than seven days. Jericho was the oldest city, the most dynamic city, and one of the leading cities in the world. It was through praise that time collapsed, and the wall fell. God worked through the obedience of His people, acting and speaking as He instructed.

In John 2, scripture describes Jesus' first recorded miracle. Jesus was in Cana of Galilee at a wedding feast, and the mother of Jesus was there. As he was there, they were running out of wine, and at that time, if you ran out of wine, you were not a good host. This would be a mark on the family. Mary loved this family, so she called on Jesus to perform a miracle. Jesus responded to her that it was not yet the time. In the King James Version, the Greek word translated as "time" is "Kairos". Mary then turns to the servants, telling them, whatever he tells you to do, do it. In this miracle, Jesus, Mary, and the disciples had entered the "miracle zone." They were in a place where God could show what could be done in a moment of Kairos. Six stone water pots stood there for Jewish custom purification, containing two or three measures each. Jesus instructed them to fill the pots with water. The pots were filled to the brim. Jesus then instructed the servants to draw some out and to bring it to the head waiter, so the servants did as they were told. Not only was the water turned to wine, but John 2:10 in the Message reads, "You've saved the best [wine] till now!" When you obey his command, time stops, and faith starts.

If we take a step back from this specific miracle and just examine the process of manufacturing wine, it demonstrates the depth of this Kairos miracle. When you plant a vine, you let it grow. You must wait several years, allowing the first good harvest to come. Even then, you do not use those grapes to make wine. You would continue to wait for subsequent harvests and, from there, could gather the juice from the harvested grapes, let it turn into the best wine, and finally bring it to the table to pour a glass and drink. God was able to work outside our "Chronos expectations!"

Time collapsed. Not only that, but God took a "non-ingredient"—something that did not have value in the process, and used it to make wine. You may not have the "right ingredients" in your next season. You may not even have what you need to make it happen in the next season, but God says, I'll take something you've got. If you'll put it in my hand, I'll turn it into what you need. 2 Peter 3:8b reminds us, "With the Lord, one day is like a thousand years, and a thousand years is like one day." (NASB 2020) God was not bound by the natural process; a moment of Kairos resulted in a miracle at the wedding feast and foreshadowed the future works of Christ.

Has there been a "Kairos moment" for you in one season that has built your faith to believe in Him for the next season? Jesus' second miracle was performed in Cana. John 4, starting in verse 46, talks about Jesus returning to Cana at Galilee, the same location where he had turned the water into wine. There was a royal official there whose Son was sick at Capernaum. This official had heard that Jesus was back and was knowledgeable of what Jesus had done the last time He was there. The official went to Jesus and began asking him to come to heal his Son, for the boy was at the point of death. This man was concerned about running out of time for his Son to be healed; however, God and his miracles are not bound by this Chronos time. Jesus pointed out that unless people see signs and wonders, they will not believe; however, he looked the official in the eyes and told him simply, "Go, your Son is alive." (v. 50 NASB 2020)

The man believed the word that Jesus spoke to him and went home. As he was going to his home, his slaves met him, saying his Son was alive. The royal official inquired of them the hour he began to get better, and they told him yesterday at the seventh hour that the fever left him; the Father knew that it was in that moment, that Kairos moment, which the miracle had occurred. It was the time at which Jesus said to him, your Son is alive. This second miracle, in which the child was at the point of death, occurred at a distance. Capernaum was 25 miles away. Within the first two miracles, Jesus demonstrated that He could collapse time and space. He can transcend and manipulate time and distance to bring you to a higher and broader place in a shorter time. Neither time nor distance was an obstacle for God.

Often in our lives, we imagine and anticipate how God will answer our prayers. Consider Mary and Martha in John 11, when their brother became ill and died. When he arrived at Jerusalem, Jesus found that Lazarus had already been in the tomb for four days. Mary and Martha were troubled, asking Jesus why He had not returned sooner. Their expectation had been for Lazarus to be healed from his illness; however, this is not the way God chose to answer this prayer and perform the miracle. Although naturally, Lazarus' body would have already started to decompose, God's Kairos time allowed Lazarus to come forth, out of the tomb, and live.

GOD IS ALWAYS ON TIME

Faith supersedes time. You can't be in faith and operating on time. We are charged with developing our relationship with him to the point where it goes beyond honoring him merely for what he does but is based on who He is. We must trust Him even in situations where it's black as midnight and we don't see a way out. We are living in this world, and things will happen in our lives. When your mind is fixed on Chronos time, you may think God's late, but He's not. God is always on time. God will always show up at your house right when you need him. Why does he do that? So he can get the glory. God will get the glory out of your situation. You're about to have a glory story! You didn't think it could be resurrected. But God said, don't worry, I will raise it. You didn't think God could turn it around, but don't worry; God is about to give you the turnaround on the worst interstate you've ever been in your life. And you're about to be headed in the right direction. God's about to take hold of your family, finances, and future. He's about to turn something around in your life. But one thing we have to learn is that if we trust him, if we just hold on and we believe in God, we can trust Him for the results.

In an excerpt from Kenneth E. Hagin's book, "*I Believe In Visions*," Jesus told Brother Hagin that this is the last great revival. He went on to say, "All the gifts of the Spirit will be in operation in the church in these last days, and the church will do greater things than even the Early Church did. It will have greater power, signs, and wonders than were recorded in the Acts of the Apostles." He said that we have seen and experienced many healings, but we will now behold amazing miracles that have not been seen before. Jesus continued, "More and more miracles will be performed in the last days which are just ahead, for it is time for the gift of the working of miracles." He stated, "Many of My people will not accept the moving of My Spirit and will turn back and will not be ready to meet Me at My coming. Many will be deceived by false prophets and miracles of satanic origin. But follow the Word of God, the Spirit of God, and Me, and you will not be deceived. I am gathering My own together and am preparing them, for the time is short." (Hagin, 2010)

YOUR KAIROS MOMENTS

You have access to Kairos moments. You have been given opportunities. If God's given you time, you can start to work without hindrance. You must embrace it as a God-given gift and fervently seek to fulfill what he's called you to do. Think of how many people you knew or times in your own life when there was a remarkable opportunity to do something amazing, tremendous, or stupendous, but you did not take advantage of the moment. God has Kairos moments ahead of us. You must let go of your disappointment and delayed dreams to reach those moments. You need to begin to hope and trust again. You must be willing to act—to say "NO!" to the devil's lies and to say a "YES!" to the promises of God! To see everything God has for us, we must begin to seize every Kairos moment.

Our God is a limitless God. He is neither limited by the changeability of your past nor the unpredictability of your future. If you consider the past, the present, and the future, God can bring everything into the right now so we can take advantage of this moment. Your preparation and Chronos' time meet in Kairos' strategic time. Regrets of the past are merely fears of the future. Throughout your life, he first wants you to know that while you might feel that you are bound by time, He is not bound by time. He is the Alpha and Omega, the beginning and the end. Perhaps doctors have said you have to go through several rounds of chemotherapy. Cancer can be in your body, and the next thing you know, it's lying in a heap on the floor. Maybe you are recovering from a serious accident. The doctors may have said it will take many months; the Lord can compress the time needed to accomplish the whole process.

Time is a precious gift. Opportunities for the kingdom are open doors provided by God Himself. God has opened doors, and sometimes we waste the opportunity. Are you prepared for the next time God brings you an opportunity to see Him move in your life? You need to prepare and pursue the calling that God has for you. As you do, your assignment, anointing, and mantle will flow together. There is always a purpose in the preparation. You will see great days in your life as long as you take the steps to pursue and prepare for it. You were born for such a time as this (Esther 4:14). Just like Esther: if not us, then who? We have access to so many miracles accounted for in the scripture. It is time for us to step into a Kairos moment.

God can set you out in a spot, in a moment, and you are involved in His move in that moment. We need to seek that Kairos moment by preparation of heart and mind so that we may be Spirit-filled for the finishing of the great work of God. When you obey his command, time stops, and faith starts. When you step out of what you can do and into what He can do, God can work Kairos miracles. We need to seek that Kairos moment by preparation of heart and mind so that we may be Spirit-filled for the finishing of the great work of God. Oral Roberts said, "Every day, miracles come to you or go past you!" We must become skillful at cooperating with miracle power so miracles don't pass us by. We must believe in the Kairos moment, the God factor, every day!

"For if you keep silent at this time,

relief and deliverance shall arise for

the Jews from elsewhere, but you and your

father's house will perish. And who knows

that you have come to the kingdom for such

a time as this and for this very occasion?"

— ESTHER 4:14 (AMPC)

CHAPTER 3

OPEN DOOR

Many people go through life without the expectation that good things can and will happen to them. I have made it a habit to remain positive and expect God's favor to be evident in my life. I learned a long time ago that when God reveals a truth in His word to you, that revelation can cause you to become positive. As we seek God to lead us daily, we are given opportunities for greatness and success. The Merriam-Webster dictionary defines opportunity as "a combination of circumstances favorable for a purpose." These opportunities typically require elements from us: areas of character development or walking in obedience to what He is instructing us to do. We can consider these instances to be God opening the door to a Kairos moment.

I believe God is calling us to prepare for every opportunity He provides us. You must be willing to step out when a God-given opportunity shows up. Ephesians 5:16 (AMP) "Making the very most of your time [on earth, recognizing and taking advantage of each opportunity and using it with wisdom and diligence], because the days are [filled with] evil." As followers of Christ, we must keep our eyes open to the work He desires us to be a part of.

"The secret to success is to be ready for the opportunities that come into your life" Benjamin Disraeli.

Many people want the success that others have, but they are not willing to do what others have done to seize the opportunity. God always has a purpose for what He does; God's purpose for opening doors of opportunity is so that He will be glorified in everything we do. These opportunities will require courage and preparation to become a reality.

COURAGE

For God's people to be used in divine opportunities and open doors, courage is a trait we must work to possess. Courage is, "the mental or moral strength to venture, persevere, and withstand danger, fear, or difficulty" (Merriam Webster). The book of Ruth in the Old Testament describes a woman who could walk forward with courage to the open door God had given her. Not only did Ruth find favor working in the field, but she was also encouraged to take a bold step, approaching Boaz directly to communicate her availability for marriage. God blessed her as she walked in obedience and courage, which also blessed others around her.

Paul's life as a follower of Jesus in the New Testament confirmed his ability to walk in courage and be an encouragement to those around him. As Paul spent time in prison, he declared that he was content in all things. (Phil 4:11). In

Acts 16, Paul and Silas prayed and sang hymns to God during an earthquake. Immediately, all jail doors were opened, and chains were unfastened. When the jailer awoke to discover what had happened, his response was to kill himself. In verse 28, "But Paul cried out with a loud voice saying, 'Do not harm yourself, for we are all here!'" (NASB 2020). If freedom had been the focus for Paul and Silas during their time in jail, the occurrence of their shackles falling off and prison doors opening would have been an answer to prayer! Instead, they remained in the prison with the others, and the result was the guard receiving his salvation! Although in this example we see literal "open doors," they had the courage and trusted in their Savior to know that He would provide; instead, this answer to prayer created an open door for the guard to be saved. Philippians 1:14 (NASB 2020) says "and that most of the brothers and the sisters trusting in the Lord because of my imprisonment have more courage to speak the word of God without fear." The ability to persevere and walk in the direction God is directing you results in testimony of courage and opens doors for God to continue His work.

We can also see how courage can help us rely on our abilities and appreciate how God adds to what we cannot do. Genesis 6 begins the story of God instructing Noah to build the ark, for the time would come when He would flood the earth. On the surface, this comes across as such an odd assignment, given that Noah had never experienced rain at this time! God gave Noah specific instructions on how to build the Ark. Noah could walk in obedience to what God was telling him, even in the face of doubt and ridicule from others. In Genesis 7:1-3, God added to the explanation, instructing Noah on which animals to bring, the quantity of each, and the timeframe for the rain to come. Noah followed God's directions, walking in courage as much of this he had never experienced and had no basis of understanding. The animals arrived for Noah to add to the ark, the rains came, and Noah's family remained safe based on the instructions from God. Noah's human ability had limits, and God supplemented them with what He could do. God had an open door for Noah to lead his family through, and Noah obeyed the call on his life! Noah was in a situation where strength was required to persevere, accomplishing what God had called him to.

PREPARATION

Paul and Silas were prepared before being imprisoned, walking in peace and finding contentment no matter their situation. Noah's relationship with God resulted in his ability to hear the direction and walk in obedience. I must be prepared to handle what is in front of me. To prepare in Strong's Dictionary can be defined as, "to be firm, stable, established, set up, ready, to make arrangement." Establishing your foundation in God by having a relationship with Him and developing the ability to hear what He has to say to you are your first steps toward being prepared. When a Christian has a strong foundation, they are ready to be used by God. The book of Esther describes a young woman who, according to custom, spent a year in a season of preparation. Following the year of preparation, God gave her an opportunity to stand. A door was opened for Esther; although the cost of that opportunity could have been death for her and her people, Esther requested a pardon for the Jewish people. Esther 4:14 (AMPC) says, "For if you keep silent at this time, relief and deliverance shall arise for the Jews from elsewhere, but you and your father's house will perish. And who knows that you have come to the kingdom for such a time as this and for this very occasion?" God had an established plan and purpose for Esther, and through preparation, the door was opened for her; Esther was obedient to walk through the door, and God was able to use Esther for His glory.

We know from scripture that while Jesus is fully God, He also walked on the earth as a man. In Philippians 2:6-7 the Bible says that He had already existed in the form of God, but also took on the form of human. Part of His time on earth was in a season of preparation. In Luke 2, we can read of Jesus growing, becoming strong, and increasing in wisdom. Later in the chapter, in verse 46, it says that Jesus was sitting among the teachers, listening and asking questions. Jesus was studying and learning to become prepared prior to the beginning of His formal ministry. John 9:4-5 (NASB 2020) says, "We must carry out the works of him who sent me as long as it's day; night is coming when no man can work. While I'm in the world, I'm the light of the world." Jesus was saying, "I'm prepared." Your assignment, anointing, and your mantle will flow together, and you will see great days in your life as long as you begin to pursue it. If you want better in your life, you need to be teachable now, allowing yourself to be prepared for the purpose He is calling you.

Once you are prepared, if you walk forward with confidence, then your courage will be contagious. When God's people take hold of this thought, God is going to raise his church back up. When you have courage, resisting fear can encourage other Christians; I believe we've all experienced this somehow. I know there have been people in my life who have encouraged me. One person whom I have looked up to is my Pastor, Pastor Rod Parsley. I told Pastor one time on the phone that, "I'm thankful for all the hell you've gone through" It reminds me that what I've faced pales in comparison, and you're still preaching, and you're still standing, and you're still doing what you're doing. I follow Pastor Parsley's example, understanding the necessity of seeking the Lord to be trained and prepared for His use. I know that even in the hell he has walked through, he has not stopped pushing forward for the sake of the Gospel.

OPPORTUNITIES TO HEAR AND RESPOND

God creates an open door—this is an opportunity for you to walk through. God does not seize opportunities; He creates them, but it is up to you to seize them. Seize means "to take possession of" something or "to take hold of" it. (Merriam Webster) It requires something to be understood fully and distinctly. As mentioned previously, John 9:4 specifies that work will not always be available to us as Christians. This verse is incredibly important because it contains a strong admonition for every serious Christian. The attitude of Jesus expressed in this scripture must also be our attitude. The AMPC translation's wording is "We must work the works of Him." The word "must" is the Greek word "dei," which carries the idea of an obligation or a necessity. This reveals that

Jesus urgently and strongly felt there was no option. It was imperative, essential, and mandatory that He properly use His time to reach souls.

Opportunities for the kingdom are open doors provided by God himself. God has opened doors for you, and there are times when you have allowed the opportunity to pass you by. But God declared over you in Joel 2:25-27 (KJV), "And I will restore to you the years that the locust hath eaten, the canker-worm and the caterpillar, and the palmerworm, my great army which I sent among you. And ye shall eat in plenty and be satisfied, and praise the name of the Lord your God, that hath dealt wondrously with you; and my people shall never be ashamed."Therefore, God has given you a space of time when you could begin to work without a hindrance in your life.

"Success occurs when opportunity meets preparation."
— ZIG ZIGLAR

Time is a precious gift. We want to ensure that the "vapor" of time we have in our lives is used for the kingdom's good. We have been mandated to carry on from where Jesus left off as He was here on earth and gave us all the tools neces-sary to continue. Do not allow your flesh to lead you past the opportunities God is giving you.

Ephesians 5:15-16 (MSG): Don't waste your time on useless work, mere busywork, the barren pursuits of darkness. Expose these things for the sham they are. It's a scandal when people waste their lives on things they must do in the dark-ness that no one will see. Rip the cover off those frauds and see how attractive they look in the light of Christ. Wake up from your sleep, climb out of your coffins, Christ will show you the light!" So, watch your step. Use your head. Make the most out of every chance you get. Walk through the doors that open before you that we may do the "greater things" as we have been charged with. In Luke 19:13, they are told, "Occupy till I come." "Occupy" in Greek is pragmateuomai, which Strong's Dictionary notes can mean "to busy oneself", "to carry on a business". (Strong's Dictionary) Thinking over your day-to-day life, we all have tasks and habits that offer no eternal purpose. God can close the doors to distraction and every time-wasting demonic influence in your life. He can close the door to everything that pulls you out of your purpose. God has a plan, purpose, mission, and goal for you. These plans have importance in light of eternity. These are desperate times!

One aspect of the desperation of these times is that, as followers of Christ, we must understand the need for people to be saved. The Great Commission in Matthew 28:19-20 commands us to make disciples—not just converts. So, the church's primary functions are to invite unbelievers to believe in Jesus for eternal life and then to invite believers to follow Jesus in this life. This entire process is called "salvation" in the Bible, and it is not just about how to go to heaven when you die, but also how to serve God and others while you live on earth. The church must tell people how to be saved so that they can serve. The church is God's hands, feet, and voice, and people primarily learn about God's love for them by how well the church functions in this world. The church also has another function: to teach and train those who believe in Jesus. God designed His church as a place where all believers can be taught God's Word and given opportunities to practice it.

Think of how many people you know who were given a remarkable opportunity to do something tremendous but failed to take advantage of the moment. This may be due to laziness, hesitation, fear, or a "take it easy" mentality. The opportunity was given to those people, but it was slipped away and lost.

A good friend of mine had given me a watch, and it meant a lot to me. I hadn't seen him in a long time. The watch was important to me, not just because of its monetary value, but also because of who gave it to me. I wore that watch several times. I was sitting in the tabernacle recently, and I had that watch on. The Lord said I want you to give that watch to that man before you. He said, I want you to give that watch to him right now. We were in service, so usually, I would wait until an opportune time when I wasn't interrupting, but the Lord said, I want you to do it right now.

I just took the watch off my wrist and put it on his. I looked at him and told him, it's your time; the time is now. I later found out that his wife, about 30 seconds before that, had sent him a text, and the text said, "God is redeeming the time in your life. God is restoring years that the enemy has stolen for you right now." When you hear God's voice, your gift can set someone in faith. Your gift at the right moment can set somebody's life in the direction of faith that they've never been in this moment. He said, I will never forget this moment. Be quick to hear God's voice and be obedient to what he tells you. When you do, God could use you to unlock something for someone.

Let Christ use you every day in every way! God has a purpose for everything He does. He has a purpose for speaking through us to His children as He wants to encourage them. His plan is at work through His children, who are obedient to hearing His voice and walking through as a door is opened. Maybe God has given you a moment when you can work to achieve something tremendous. There could be an exceptional prospect standing before you that will enable you to make a difference in someone else's life. Like Jesus, you must give yourself enthusiastically and passionately to the task that lies before you. These opportunities are usually short-term, so you must seize the moment now while it is still day!

SEEING OUR PERSONAL DOORS OPENING

For God to work in our lives, we must remember what the Bible says in Ephesians 3:20-21 (MSG) "God can do anything, you know-far more than you could ever imagine or guess or request in your wildest dreams! He does it not by pushing us around but by working within us, his Spirit deeply and gently within us." God has already begun a work in you—and regardless of what He has done, you can begin to show gratitude, living a lifestyle of praise. Gratitude is a key that unlocks the power and His movement in your life. You need to stop complaining and remember all the good things God has done.

As you do this, it will begin to lift your spirits, giving you faith to continue believing in the blessings in your life. Psalms 50:14-15 (TPT) says, "Why don't you bring me the sacrifices I desire? Bring me your true and sincere thanks, and show your gratitude by keeping your promises to me, the Most High. Honor me by trusting in me in your day of trouble. Cry aloud to me, and I will be there to rescue you." As we praise and glorify His name, the word says that "He inhabits the praises of His people." We can expect to see God work as we praise Him.

Luke 17 shows us a very clear distinction between merely requesting healing and changing focus to praising God for what He has done. Luke 17:11 (TPT) says: "On his way to Jerusalem, Jesus passed through the border region between Samaria and Galilee. Ten men approached him as he entered one village, but they kept their distance, for they were lepers. They shouted to him, 'Mighty Lord, our wonderful Master! Won't you have mercy on us and heal us?' When Jesus stopped to look at them, he spoke these words: 'Go to be examined by the Jewish priests.' They set off, and they were healed along the way. When he discovered that he was completely healed, one of them, a Samaritan turned back to find Jesus, shouting out joyous praises and glorifying God. When he found Jesus, he fell down at his feet and thanked him repeatedly, saying, 'You are the Messiah.' 'So where are the other nine?' Jesus asked. 'Weren't there ten who were healed? They all refused to return to give thanks and give glory to God except you, a foreigner from Samaria?' Then Jesus said to the healed man lying at his feet, 'Arise and go. It was your faith that brought you salvation and made you whole.'" Only one turned back and glorified God with a loud voice, falling at His feet. Gratitude unlocks wholeness. There were ten lepers touched and healed. But only one was made whole. There is a difference between being touched, healed, and made whole. When you take up a position of gratitude, something happens in your heart.

Luke's testimony of the ten lepers describes people who were lepers but were then healed. The one who returned to Jesus' feet was made whole. Maybe you were lost and on your way to hell, but now you are saved. Maybe you were depressed, but now you have found joy. You can always find something to thank God for in your life, having a heart full of gratitude. As you praise Him and see Him move in your life, doors open for you to walk into. God will give you opportunities to walk forward into those open doors where you may participate in the work He is doing. Be sensitive to His voice and have praise always on your lips so that you can then serve God at a greater capacity every day, advancing the kingdom.

In these last days, we see doors open as God provides Kairos moments for us to walk into. God desires to open doors for us to walk through in service and obedience and bring promises to pass in our lives. Ecclesiastes 11:6 (NASB 2020) says, "Sow your seed in the morning and do not be idle in the evening, for you do not know whether morning or evening sowing will succeed, or whether both of them alike will be good." We sow seed into good ground, believing for a harvest. This harvest may be for physical healing, financial breakthroughs, business ideas, success, or miracles. Amos 9:13 (MSG) says, "Yes indeed, it won't be long now.' God's Decree. 'Things are going to happen so fast your head will swim, one thing fast on the heels of the other. You won't be able to keep up. Everything will be happening at once everywhere you look Blessings! Blessings like wine pouring off the mountains and hills.'"

When we live by faith, there are times when, to everyone else, it appears that we are taking a great risk or laying everything on the line. We also could have others come against us. Others can plant seeds of doubt, causing us to question what the word says or the promise that we are standing on. Developing our relationship with Christ, meditating on the word, and knowing how to respond to the "nay-sayers" in our lives can support our forward momentum in walking through the doors God is opening for us!

"*Therefore, since we also have such a great cloud of witnesses surrounding us, let us rid ourselves of every obstacle and the sin which so easily entangles us, and let's run with endurance the race that is set before us.*"

— Hebrews 12:1 (nasb 2020)

CHAPTER 4

MANY ADVERSARIES

Not only is the door that God has opened for you important but the door you close is just as important. Some doors need to be closed and locked. You need to make the decision never to open those doors! You will not go back that way. If you leave the door open, flies will come in, as well as bugs, pests, demons, and people. There are some cycles in your life that you keep revolving through, like a revolving door. It could look like a New Year's Resolution where you could beat this for a week or two, but by the end of January, you don't remember what you had resolved to do or not do. You end up returning to that place you had vowed to leave behind. It is easy to look at outside influences as the cause of backtracking to old habits; while sometimes it is an external factor, that is not always the case.

When I think about doors, God takes me back to my mind, heart, and mouth. These are three things you have control over. Romans 8:6 describes how the mind can waver:

"For to set the mind on the flesh is death, but to set the mind on the Spirit is life and peace." The word "mind" is defined in Strong's dictionary as "mental inclination or purpose."

We must consciously decide to keep our minds focused on the word of God and His truth. The word "heart" is used figuratively for feelings, the will, and intellect. It is used as the center of anything. We see the importance of protecting the heart in Proverbs 4:23, "Guard your heart above all else, for it determines the course of your life." As you spend time in the word, receiving revelation from the Holy Spirit, He strengthens your heart, making you less susceptible to an attack. As mentioned in Romans 8:6, he gives you the ability to set your mind on the Spirit.

Psalms 141:3 (NASB 2020) says, "Set a guard, Lord, over my mouth. Keep watch over the door of my lips." When you open your mouth, you're opening a door. Your tongue of confession leads you into possession.

As you continue to develop your relationship with God, receiving the revelation the Holy Spirit is showing you from the Word, He continues to open doors for you to walk through. As you go through those doors, however, you may have battles to face. 1 Corinthians 16:9 says, "For a great and effective door has opened to me, and there are many adversaries." It is easy to fall into a trap where you question the opportunity because of the battle you're facing. Maybe you don't believe you're even worthy of an opportunity. You don't believe God could open a door for you or that you're going anywhere. If you continue to believe along this vein, you cannot walk through the door God holds open for you. We know that based on God's character, we can trust and have faith in the opportunities He leads us to, as they are backed by His word. It is also essential to continue pushing toward those opportunities, even in the face of opposition, by speaking the truth and seeking God for further revelation.

For many years, the Lord has instructed me to say: "Change your thoughts, change your words, change your life." The thoughts that originate in your mind create either life or death as they come out of your mouth. If you don't start thinking differently, your words will never change. You need to begin to cast down imaginations and every high thing that exalts itself against the knowledge of God. (2 Cor 10:5) If you think differently, you'll begin to speak differently. If your life is going in the wrong direction, most of the time, it's not the devil's fault that you're in that situation. You could be leaving a door open. The elements you see in your life are there because they go from your head out through your mouth. Decide to close the door to anything pulling you away from the truth of God.

YOU MAY BE AN ADVERSARY

Joshua spent many years under Moses' covering; after he passed, Joshua needed to understand how to move forward now that Moses was no longer with him. God encouraged him to move through the next door and stop thinking about the last. For you to go to your next, you must let go of your past. And some of you need to tell yourself, that season is dead. It's over. This is another time when our thought life can open doors of fear or uncertainty, holding us back from walking through the open door God has for us. Joshua 1:2-3

(NASB 2020) says, "Moses, My servant is dead; so now arise, cross this Jordan, you and all these people, to the land which I am giving to them, to the sons of Israel. Every place on which the sole of your foot steps, I have given it to you, just as I spoke to Moses" God was telling Joshua, "I am passing the baton to you. Moses was a great leader, but now it's your turn to enter the life I've called you to."

Wherever you go, some things are going to have to die. There are some things you'll have to cross over away from and over into. You will need to decide that even if it is good, if God tells you to move on, you have to move on. Take any thoughts captive that question God's sovereignty or faithfulness. These could sound like thoughts encouraging you to stay in the familiar or comfortable—or even thoughts of guilt, shame, and inadequacy. These thoughts will continue to control your life and hold you back from His promises. As you are contending for your next, these are some thoughts that you may find yourself needing to cast down:

1. It's impossible.
2. It can't be done.
3. I don't have what it takes.
4. It's too risky.
5. What if it doesn't work?
6. What if I lose everything I have?

Get rid of negative thinking. Get these out of your vocabulary!

If you lose everything you have, then start over. If that happens, then what God helps you rebuild is bigger, stronger, and better than before. You'll never seize an opportunity hanging on to what you think is security. The only secure thing you and I have is the Word of God. Maintain a positive perspective and attitude and become more sensitive to the opportunities God is bringing before you.

Your future will look bright when your attitude is bright. It is evident that many of the thoughts that enter your mind are generated by your flesh with the intent to hold you back; however, the enemy also wants to keep you from moving into your next. We see several examples in the Word where Satan is influencing people, causing them to stay back or question what God has said. One of the most well-known accounts is from the very beginning of creation.

WHEN SATAN IS AN ADVERSARY

Genesis 3:1 (NLT) says, "The serpent was the shrewdest of all the wild animals the Lord God had made. One day he asked the woman, 'Did God really say you must not eat the fruit from any of the trees in the garden?'" The phrase "Did God say?" was the entry point to the mind and the heart. The mind began to question what God said. A door is opened when we question what God said. God says something about your life, and then the enemy comes in and says, "But did God really say that?" You can trust what God says. Every word that is in the Bible is true. If God said it, you can have it. You can stand on it. You can proclaim it and trust it. Anything else attempting to come in and challenge the word of God must addressed immediately. You must cast down every imagination and close the door.

In your life, the enemy only takes the opportunity you give him. He's looking for an opening. The devil and his demons cannot just come and do things to us without an open door. In 1 Peter 5:8, the Bible says, "Be sober, be vigilant because your adversary, the devil, walks about like a roaring lion, seeking an open door, seeking whom he may devour." If you're a Christian, born-again, Spirit-filled believer, the devil cannot just come in and out of your life. You have the authority and the ability to resist his attempts. 1 Corinthians10:13 (NIV) says: "No temptation has overtaken you except what is common to mankind. And God is faithful; He will not allow you to be tempted beyond what you can bear. But when you are tempted, He will also provide a way out so that you can endure it." When we give into these questioning thoughts and yield to his suggestions, we are actually empowering the enemy. We must stop any thought that does not align with what God says before allowing it to have power in our lives.

Meditating on the Word of God means to murmur or mutter. As we meditate on what the Bible says, we change the thoughts entering our minds, affecting our words and actions. Joshua 1:8 (ESV) says, "This book of the Law shall not depart from your mouth, but you shall meditate on it day and night, so that you may be careful to do according to all written in it. For then you will make your way prosperous, and then you will have good success." Meditating on the word allows the believer to identify the thoughts that have entered the mind. As thoughts come in that don't align with the Word of God, a believer can take those thoughts captive, stopping any attack on its track.

How did David, a shepherd boy, become so strong in

Spirit that God chose him to be King of Israel? The answer comes from revelation knowledge, which turned David into a spiritual powerhouse. It was a revelation that came to him through hours of thinking about the things of God.

You can almost imagine the day he wrote Psalm 23; maybe he was just sitting and singing praises to God, meditating on His goodness. He was just fellowshipping with Him when suddenly the Anointing of the Lord came upon him, and he realized, "The Lord is *my* Shepherd!" (Psalm 23) Suddenly, he thought about the sheep he watched over as a boy; I faced death for those sheep. I led them where pastures were green, and the waters were cool, clean, deep, and peaceful. Maybe he continued to meditate on that word as it thrilled him. *When the lion and the bear came, didn't God prepare a table before me in the presence of those enemies? He gave me victory! My God! My God will fight for me! The Lord is my Shepherd, and I shall not want!* This revelation would have been so strong that the devil couldn't beat it out of him. So, when Goliath tried to make a fool out of Israel, David went after him. Goliath could scare off everyone else but couldn't shake David because he had a revelation inside of him that said, "Though I walk through the valley of the shadow of death, I will fear no evil; for my, God is with me."

That revelation enabled David to say, "I came against you in the name of the Lord of Hosts (1 Samuel 17:45)," and send a rock sailing into the giant's brain. Revelation knowledge is your key to victory that will help you resist any attack that would prevent you from walking into God's open door.

INFLUENCE FROM OTHERS

Similar to Eve's experience with the serpent in Genesis, you may be walking in faith and holding onto revelation knowledge from God. Other people may try to interfere with the promise you're believing in. Bartimaeus experienced this when he believed in his miracle.

Mark 10:46-52 (NASB 2020) says, "Then they came to Jericho. And later, as He was leaving Jericho with His disciples and a large crowd, a better who was blind named Bartimaeus, the son of Timaeus was sitting by the road. And when he heard that it was Jesus the Nazarene, he began to cry out and say, 'Jesus, Son of David, have mercy on me!' Many sternly told him to be quiet, but he kept crying out, 'Son of David, have mercy on me!' And Jesus stopped and said, 'Call him here.' So they called the man who was blind, saying to him, 'Take courage, stand up! He is calling for you.' And throwing off his cloak, he jumped up and came to Jesus. And replying to him, Jesus said, 'What do you want Me to do for you?' And the man who was blind said to Him, 'Rabboni, I want to regain my sight!' And Jesus said to him, 'Go; your faith has made you well.' And immediately he regained his sight and began following Him on the road."

Notice, in the text, as Bartimaeus was yelling for Jesus, "Be quiet" was what many people yelled at him. When you say that God will make a way when there seems to be no way, people will try to shut you up. The devil knew there was about to be an advancement, and the last thing he would want was for people to see a miraculous move by Christ. It wasn't just critics or skeptics standing there, trying to silence

Bartimaeus—it was also the religious crowd. The disciples said things like, "You're speaking out of turn." They tried to reign him back from reaching out to Jesus. "Instead of complying, Bartimaeus only started yelling louder. Not only is the outside influence trying to silence the church, but the church is also trying to silence the church.

The scripture also shows us that the crowd changes—it will always go with the flow. The people before saying "be quiet" now say "cheer up"—they will shift like the wind, but you need to stay the course. You may be down to having only one resource—your voice. God will stop everything; the time will stop clicking on. God's calling you into something greater. You cannot allow outside forces to take your ground. Some people let a church speak negatively about what you believe God for, so they begin to back off from declarations or to believe God. In that situation, you're listening to men more than listening to God. You're allowing human pressure to hold you back. Some bible translations say that people rebuked Bartimaeus. Rebuke means to express sharp disapproval or criticism (Merriam Webster). These people, who are trying to convince you to silence your mind and walk away from your passion, are in the church and in the world. They represent both the saved and the lost people of the world. Their main goal is for you to shut up and follow suit with the crowd.

Bartimaeus' call unlocked a miracle for him; instead of being silenced, he continued to speak in faith for the move of God. There is a sound in your voice; when you release it, your voice will help propel you forward. Jesus will wait for you to get into his presence. If Bartimaeus had remained on his mat, sitting in silence, he would not have received his miracle at that moment. Complacency will silence you. Where and when you sit down and remain silent, you continue to stay.

RESISTING THE ADVERSARY

We know we have adversaries. Forces rise up against us to stop us from entering the door God has opened for us. I want to equip you with some key points to consider as you prepare to walk into the promises He has for you.

1. Don't let anybody silence your voice or dampen your enthusiasm when you're chasing after Jesus. This mostly happens in religious settings. Bartimaeus was blind, So He would not have been able to walk through a crowd looking for Jesus. He only had one resource: his voice. If you get your mouth to line up with God's word and get faith in your mouth, you can start speaking into your future.

2. Your relationship with Christ is personal. Like Bartimaeus, we need to focus on God and Him only. We have a race to run. We can only do that when we focus on the path set before us and not get distracted by what people say to us or about us.

3. Being baptized in the Holy Spirit with the evidence of speaking in tongues can provide the believer with opportunities to pray and intercede, while the prayer remains a secret from the adversary. This is a time when you can pray in line with the Holy Spirit, praying according to His perfect will, and know with confidence that it will thwart attempts from the adversary to interfere with your prayer.

4. Obstacles will be put in your way; be ready to cast things aside. Hebrews 12:1 (NASB 2020) says:
   "Therefore, since we also have such a great cloud of witnesses surrounding us, let us rid ourselves of every obstacle and the sin which so easily entangles us, and let's run with endurance the race that is set before us."

There's a race, a journey, a path—set before us. Seek God for what He wants to do in your life and His calling in your life. That is your lane. Cast aside every weight. What you're facing may not look like joy, but with joy, you need to face it. Like blind Bartimaeus, we must decide to pursue God even when things get in our way. We don't need to fall victim when we face an attack from an adversary; instead, we can meditate on the Word of God. We can take captive any thought that does not align with the word and claim victory as we walk through the open doors that He has waiting! With praise and a shout, walk right into what you are called to do!

"The Spirit, not content to flit around on the surface, dives into the depths of God, and brings out what God planned all along. Who ever knows what you're thinking and planning except you yourself? The same with God—except that he not only knows what he's thinking, but he lets us in on it. God offers a full report on the gifts of life and salvation that he is giving us. We don't have to rely on the world's guesses and opinions. We didn't learn this by reading books or going to school; we learned it from God, who taught us person-to-person through Jesus and we're passing it on to you in the same firsthand, personal way."

— 1 Corinthians 2:10b-13

CHAPTER 5

FULLNESS OF PREPARATION

We know from scripture that we have a very short amount of time to be obedient to God's call on our life, the mantle He has called us to carry and accomplish the tasks He has for us to do. Some of that time is set aside as a time of preparation. The meaning of the word "preparation" is "the action or process of making something ready." (Merriam Webster) There are times in scripture when this preparation process is very short and other times when it is accomplished over decades; however, we know that God has a plan and a purpose for everything He does. By obeying His leading, we can walk into the fullness of preparation and, in turn, can expect to see God working all things together, even resulting in miracles and "suddenly" coming to pass! As we develop a clear understanding and revelation of the word of God, we can begin to understand the importance of preparation to walk into everything God has for us and into our destiny!

THE VIEW OF THE WORD

A Biblical worldview, also called a Christian worldview, is built upon the framework of ideas and beliefs through which a Christian individual or group interprets the world and interacts with the world. Our worldview shapes our physical, emotional, intellectual, and spiritual dimensions. The most important worldview element is how questions are answered about God.

As Franklin Graham wrote in an article titled, "A Biblical Worldview in Today's Culture", "The Biblical worldview says there is a God—One who is personal, powerful, and caring—who created the world and everything in it. It states unequivocally that man is created in God's image, living in essence as God's co-regent over creation. Mankind—born and unborn, rich and poor, able and disabled—has intrinsic worth. Almighty God is a sovereign God, ruler over nations, states, empires, and governments. He is to be worshipped and obeyed through the precepts and principles revealed in His infallible Word. He not only exists, but He is sovereign over all of history according to His wisdom and purposes. He is intimately involved in every aspect of life." (Franklin Graham, "A Biblical Worldview in Today's Culture") Unfortunately, our current society is trying to affect how people view the Word of God.

Given the explanation of a Biblical or Christian world-view, the assumption would be that a church that professes to be "Christian" or "Bible-believing" would maintain that God is infallible and that He is the same yesterday, today, and forever. The Bible would remain the Word of God and be upheld as the standard to which the church would develop its statement of faith. One popular trend happening now in many churches is the modification of the belief system and standards to be more accommodating and affirming to the culture in society. Denominations are publicizing their alterations to long-standing traditions because of the pressure from the mainstream opinions in our culture. Division in the church results in the inability to provide a consistent answer to the world about who God is.

Outside of the church, we are living in a world where men and women are allowed to use restrooms or dressing rooms based on their own chosen identity, male or female. Children are encouraged from a young age to decide which gender, if any, to identify. Abortions are increasing, and according to a study by the Guttmacher Institute, it is estimated that over 878,000 abortions occurred in the 10-month period between January and October, 2023. (Guttmacher Institute, 2024, January 17) Our culture boasts the "right" to worship anything or anyone, believing that it will result in the individual's desired eternity and existence outside of any accountability or consequences for the choices being made. Any opinion that is counter to the worldview is seen as being "phobic," and many assume that you, in turn, hate the individual. This popular worldview gives no acknowledgment to the Word of God.

In a 2022 poll from Gallup, "a record-low 20% of Americans now say the Bible is the literal word of God, down from 24% the last time the question was asked in 2017 and half of what it was at its high points in 1980 and 1984. Meanwhile, a new high of 29% says the Bible is a collection of 'fables, legends, history and moral precepts recorded by man.' This marks the first time significantly more Americans have viewed the Bible as not divinely inspired, as opposed to the literal word of God." (Newport, 2002, July 6) Even though more than two thousand years have passed, Paul describes in 1 Corinthians how the reality of God—who He is, why Jesus came to dwell among us, and the truth that He established, is not what the world teaches.

Paul's cry mirrors the way that our society regards our Savior. In 1 Corinthians 2:6-10a in the Message Bible, he explains:

"We, of course, have plenty of wisdom to pass on to you once you get your feet on firm spiritual ground, but it's not popular wisdom, the fashionable wisdom of high-priced experts that will be out-of-date in a year or so. God's wisdom is something mysterious that goes deep into the interior of his purposes. You don't find it lying around on the surface. It's not the latest message, but more like the oldest—what God determined as the way to bring out his best in us, long before we ever arrived on the scene. The experts of our day haven't a clue about what this eternal plan is. If they had, they wouldn't have killed the Master of the God-designed life on a cross. That's why we have this Scripture: No one's ever seen or heard anything like this, never so much as imagined anything quite like it—what God has arranged for those who love him. But *you've* seen or heard it because God by his Spirit has brought it all out into the open before you."

Christians, who have a revelation for who God is, seek to live a life with eternal purpose; this is contrary in many ways to the way of the world. Revelation, direction, and guidance are sought, that you would do as God desires. God has a plan and purpose, much bigger than each of us, for everything He does. Just as Paul explains in 1 Corinthians 2, we cannot understand or imagine what God has planned for His people.

There is a constant prophetic flow in scripture of preparation for the prophecy to come to pass. Things that must be obeyed, steps that must be taken, things that need to be removed, and things that must be received. Moses walked through seasons of preparation, trusting and following the leading of God that he would be used in mighty ways. The plan that God had for Moses would fulfill the words of prophecy that God had given to Abraham, Isaac, and Jacob.

A SOMEBODY TO A NOBODY

The life of Moses is a great story of preparation. There is an old saying that Moses was a "somebody" for forty years, and then a "nobody" for forty years, and then learned what God could do with "a nobody" for forty years. There is a lot of truth to this summary of Moses' life!

Moses was raised as the Grandson of the Pharaoh in the Palace of Egypt, where he was taught academic subjects and learned the art of war and leadership. He was raised in the house of a King and trained how to rule and reign. The first 40 years of his life were an amazing life in one of the greatest atmospheres of his day.

God knew the plan that He had for Moses, to lead His people out of Egypt. This plan involved leading his people through the desert; therefore, Moses had to be trained and prepared. While this could have been accomplished in different ways, God was able to use the time when Moses was exiled to teach him how to survive the hot and the cold, how to find food to eat, where to get water, and ultimately, how to exist in the desert life! Moses was eighty when he led the people of God out of Egypt. Moses led God's people in the desert for 40 years to reach the Promised Land. Doing the math, it ended up being eighty years of training for forty years of leadership!

This is one of the greatest stories of preparation that we have to glean from scripture. There were questions and frustration; however, through all that, Moses became one of the greatest leaders of men that the world has ever known! It's not too late for you; keep preparing! God is preparing you just like He did with Moses. He was preparing Moses to be the kind of person who would walk into the throne room of the most powerful King in the world and say, "Let my people go!" He was preparing him to be the kind of leader who could handle the whining and complaining of the children of Israel. He was busy preparing him in the palace and the desert. Let God accomplish the preparation so you are prepared for the next! People used to say don't get out in front of God! Trust Him in the process.

DREAMS AND VISIONS

Just like Moses, there were times in Joseph's life when he was regarded as a nobody and later seen as a somebody. When Joseph shared with his brothers the dreams and visions God was giving to him, they ended up selling him into slavery, allowing their father to believe that he had been killed. Through each shift, God remained with Joseph and was faithful to him. The manager of Pharaoh's household, Potiphar, bought Joseph from the Ishmaelites. According to Genesis 39:2, Joseph's Master recognized God's work in Joseph's life and was very fond of him. Joseph was put in charge of several aspects of his Master's life, resulting in God blessing Potipher's household. Potipher's wife then framed Joseph, and he quickly ended up in jail with the King's prisoners. Joseph was given an incredible amount of freedom and responsibility even within the jail! In verse 23, the NASB translation says: "The prison warden did not supervise anything under Joseph's authority, because the Lord was with him; and, the Lord made whatever he did prosper." (NASB 2020)

Joseph's life makes another transition because of the dreams that God interprets for him while in prison. Eventually, Pharaoh heard Joseph's ability to interpret dreams, and he called for Joseph to come to his assistance. Joseph went from prison to being a ruler of Egypt, only under Pharaoh in terms of the throne. Through the plans that God had for Joseph's life and Joseph's obedience in Genesis 45:4-8 in the Message Bible says:

"'Come closer to me,' Joseph said to his brothers. They came closer. 'I am Joseph your brother whom you sold into Egypt. But don't feel badly, don't blame yourselves for selling me. God was behind it. God sent me here ahead of you to save lives. There has been a famine in the land now for two years the famine will continue for five more years—neither plowing nor harvesting. God sent me on ahead to pave the way and make sure there was a remnant in the land, to save your lives in an amazing act of deliverance. So you see, it wasn't you who sent me here but God. He set me in place as a father to Pharaoh, put me in charge of his personal affairs, and made me ruler of all Egypt.'"

Not only was there full reconciliation between Joseph and his family because of how God prepared and led Joseph, but Joseph was also able to use his gift to help prepare the people of Egypt for the famine that was to happen. As described in Genesis, each season of Joseph's life was a time God could use as preparation. The visions and dreams Joseph experienced and the ability to interpret them were not skills that Joseph understood immediately. It was a gift that God refined to better prepare Joseph for the calling that was on his life. Romans 8:28 in the AMPC says, "And we know [with great confidence] that God [who is deeply concerned about us] causes all things to work together [as a plan] for good for those who love God, to those who are called according to His plan and purpose." It is amazing how many accounts of miracles, both in scripture and in the present day, will illustrate how much God brings different pieces together, and the result in all of it is that He gets the glory!

PREPARED FOR BATTLE

The scripture also provides us with times when the situation does not seem possible, or the assumed result will not be acquired. However, through the preparation of God, it has the best result! In 1 Samuel 17, the Bible tells the story of David, the youngest of twelve sons. When the nation was called to war, David's brothers joined the army, but the army did not engage. Part of the Philistine army was a giant named Goliath, who was said to have been over nine feet tall. Goliath would come to the front of the Philistine line each day, mocking Israel's army and their God. The Israelites remained frozen due to fear.

David's father had asked David to go to the front lines for information about his brothers. While he was there, he witnessed Israel's army fleeing away from Goliath in fear. In 1 Samuel 17:32 (MSG), it says, "'Master,' said David, 'don't give up hope. I'm ready to go and fight this Philistine.' Saul answered David, 'You can't go and fight this Philistine. You're too young and inexperienced—and he's been in this fighting business since before you were born.' David said, "I've been a shepherd, tending sheep for my father. Whenever a lion or bear came and took a lamb from the flock, I'd go after it, knock it down, and rescue the lamb. If it turned on me, I'd grab it by the throat, wring its neck, and kill it. Lion or bear, it made no difference—I killed it. And I'll do the same to this Philistine pig who is taunting the troops of God –Alive. God, who delivered me from the teeth of the lion and the claws of the bear, will deliver me from this Philistine.' Saul said, 'Go—And God help you!'"

Preparation isn't based on the outward appearance or someone else's concept of your experience and status. God accomplishes preparation and can lead you when you are ready to continue. David obeyed to complete the task he was called to, later denying the armor offered to him because it was not what he had worn to train. (v. 39). In verses 45-47 in the Message version, it says, "David answered, 'You come at me with sword and spear and battle-ax. I come at you in the name of God-of-the-Angel-Armies, the God of Israel's troops, whom you curse and mock. This very day God is handing you over to me. I'm about to kill you, cut off your head, and serve up your body and the bodies of your Philistine buddies to the crows and coyotes. The whole earth will know that there's an extraordinary God in Israel. And everyone gathered here will learn the God doesn't save by means of sword or spear. The battle belongs to God—he's handing you to us on a platter!"

God had called David forward from herding sheep, a season in which He was training and preparing him for service. David recognized the call on his life, was anointed for service, and was willing to be obedient even when, in the natural, the odds were stacked against him. David had the confidence from God that he was prepared and ready for this fight, resulting in a victory—not only for his country but also for the God he loved! This stance was not in line with either his family or his community. David didn't depend on their validation to move forward in what he knew from God. We see traces of this every day in our world.

A CHANGING SOCIETY

Our society is changing and becoming more and more focused on non-traditional lifestyles and people following the desires of their flesh. We have a living, breathing word that leads us to the truth of salvation. God has given us the tools we need to be prepared to walk into the fullness He has for us; we are accountable for doing our part to see that come to pass. In 1 Corinthians 2:10b-13, it says:

"The Spirit, not content to flit around on the surface, dives into the depths of God, and brings out what God planned all along. Who ever knows what you're thinking and planning except you yourself? The same with God—except that he not only knows what he's thinking, but he lets *us* in on it. God offers a full report on the gifts of life and salvation that he is giving us. We don't have to rely on the world's guesses and opinions. We didn't learn this by reading books or going to school; we learned it from God, who taught us person-to-person through Jesus and we're passing it on to you in the same firsthand, personal way."

Christians are to hold the Word of God in the highest esteem, realizing how vital it is in the believer's life. As the Gallop poll describes, our society has a gross misunderstanding of the Bible's significance, similar to Paul's warnings to Timothy.

Paul warns Timothy to handle the word of God accurately. 2 Timothy 2:16-19 says, "But avoid worldly and empty chatter, for it will lead to further ungodliness, and their talk will spread like gangrene. Among them are Hymenaeus and Philetus, men who have gone astray from the truth, claiming that the resurrection has already taken place and they are jeopardizing the faith of some. Nevertheless, the firm foundation of God stands, having this seal: The Lord knows those who are His; and, everyone who names the name of the Lord is to keep away from wickedness." The Doctrine of the resurrection being the very keystone of Christianity, we are told clearly from these verses that the world will not prepare us to walk in the fullness of preparation for what God is calling us to. We need to seek God through His word and pray for the Holy Spirit to give us revelation of the direction we are to go.

I encourage you to resist the mindset of being stuck in a season of preparation and feeling that you have yet to arrive in the place God is calling you to. It is a tendency to be influenced by people and voices that you're surrounded by and also focus on the concept of time that we live by, the rules of Chronos time. We allow those influences to start a voice of doubt, considering the results if God's promises are not "yes and amen." I believe we are walking into a time when these pieces will come together in Kairos moments that our minds cannot comprehend. That one moment, you will be in your now, and the next, you've reached the fullness of preparation, and you're walking into your future. Keep a hold on the word of God, continue to walk in the preparation He is leading you in, and open your eyes to see the "suddenlies" coming to pass around you!

"Not that I have already obtained all this, or have already arrived at my goal, but I press on to take hold of that for which Christ Jesus took hold of me. Brothers and sisters, I do not consider myself yet to have taken hold of it. But one thing I do: Forgetting what is behind and straining toward what is ahead, I press on toward the goal to win the prize for which God has called me heavenward in Christ Jesus."

— PHILIPPIANS 3:12-14 (KJV)

CHAPTER 6

✦━━━ ━ ━━━✦

FULLNESS OF TIME

It is common for a believer to receive a prophetic word or a vision from the Lord of something that is promised to happen, only to then wait and wonder what the time frame is or even if it will ever happen! When we receive healing or a promise in the Spirit, we pray into the time when we can hold it in the natural. We say things like something will happen "some time"; however, a deeper meaning involves steps and cooperation that lead you to something coming to pass. If you say that something will happen in the fullness of time, you mean that it will eventually happen after a long time or a long series of events; however, I want to try to bring some revelation to the thoughts about time from a biblical perspective.

In the garden of Gethsemane, a very short time before Jesus was to be taken and crucified, He made a very simple request of his disciples. Matthew 26:41 (AMPC) says, "All of you must keep awake (give strict attention, be cautious and active) and watch and pray, that you may not come into temptation. The Spirit indeed is willing, but the flesh is weak." Jesus was requesting those with Him to watch and pray. Watching means, you have to be aware of times and seasons. Prayer is communication and working with the Lord to see His will orchestrated in the earth. God is working out His eternal plan; at times, we are completely in the dark about what is happening. So we watch, pray, and allow the Holy Spirit to reveal what's happening now!

GOD KEEPS HIS WORD

In Genesis 3:15, which you may consider as the first Gospel, God promised, "And I will put enmity Between you and the woman, and between your seed and her Seed; He shall bruise your head, And you shall bruise His heel." This is one of the first prophecies we see in scripture that refers to the coming of Christ.

God promised Adam and all of mankind that the Redeemer would come. And this Redeemer would bruise the head of the serpent Satan and provide atonement for the sin of the fallen mankind. It was promised that this Messiah would come from the lineage of Abraham, Isaac, and Jacob— and from the Tribe of Judah. When you read the Gospel of Matthew and the genealogy of Christ, you confirm from the family tree that all that was said about Jesus came to pass.

It was promised or prophesied that He will be the heir to the throne of David in Isaiah 9:6-7.

"For unto us a Child is born, Unto us a Son is given; And the government will be upon His shoulder. And His name will be called Wonderful, Counselor, Mighty God, Everlasting Father, Prince of Peace. Of the increase of His government and peace There will be no end, Upon the throne of David and over His kingdom, To order it and establish it with judgment and justice From that time forward, even forever. The zeal of the Lord of hosts will perform this."

When the fullness of the time had come, God sent forth His Son, born of a woman, born under the law, to redeem those under the law, that we might receive the adoption as sons. And because you are sons, God has sent forth the Spirit of His Son into your hearts, crying out, "Abba, Father!" Therefore, you are no longer a slave but a son, and if you are a son, then you are an heir of God through Christ. Galatians 4:4-7 (NKJV)

The account in Luke 1:31-33 tells us that this promise was fully fulfilled. In the Book of Micah—Micah the Prophet 5: the exact place of HIS birth was mentioned by this prophet.

"But you, Bethlehem Ephrathah, Though you are little among the thousands of Judah, Yet out of you shall come forth to Me The One to be Ruler in Israel, Whose goings forth are from of old, From everlasting." Micah 5:2 (NKJV)

Do you see that? The prophet mentioned that Bethlehem would be the birthplace of our Lord Jesus Christ! Mary and Joseph had to travel to Bethlehem at exactly the right moment in time. The Roman emperor had ordered that a census, or record, of all people be taken in their hometown. It was that exact moment that brought about the fullness of time. The fullness of time reaches back to eternity past and stretches to the Kairos moment of now and eternity of the future.

Luke records that Mary and Joseph traveled to Bethlehem—a City of David: there, she delivered Jesus in a manger. What does all this leave us with? The promises were kept in the fullness of time; the prophecies were fulfilled. God never fails. All that our Lord Jesus did during His earthly life was to fulfill promises and prophecies in the fullness of time. Similar to believing for the fullness of time to come to pass in the birth of Jesus, Abraham was also given a prophetic word that would not be fulfilled within his lifetime.

PROPHECY AND OBEDIENCE

In Genesis 12:7, God calls Abraham to build an altar in a specific place, promising the land to his descendants. Abraham knew that it was not a land that he would see for himself, and in Genesis 15:13-14, the Bible says, "Know for certain that your descendants will be strangers in a land that is not theirs, where they will be enslaved and oppressed for four hundred years. But I will also judge the nation they will serve, and afterward, they will come out with many possessions."

He gives the promise in verse 18, which says, "On that day the Lord made a covenant with Abram, saying, 'To your descendants, I have given this land, From the river of Egypt as far as the great river, the river Euphrates." He confirms this promise as he declares to Isaac in Genesis 26:3-5, which says, "Live for a time in this land, and I will be with you and bless you, for to you and your descendants I will give all these lands, and I will establish the oath which I swore to your father, Abraham. I will multiply your descendants as the stars of heaven and will give your descendants all these lands, and by your descendants, all the nations of the earth shall be blessed." In Genesis 28:15-17, God declares to Jacob, "Behold, I am with you and will keep you wherever you go, and bring you back to this land; for I will not leave you until I have done what I promised you. Then Jacob awoke from his sleep and said, 'The Lord is certainly in this place, and I did not know it!'" The Bible describes this land as "flowing with milk and honey," with rich soil, security from the mountains, and protection. Similar to the character of God, obedience to His direction would provide them with everything they need.

When Moses led the Israelites out of Egypt to the Promised Land, we know from scripture that God was faithful and provided for their needs from the beginning of their journey. They witnessed miracles of the parting of the Red Sea, seeing Moses' staff turn into a snake and return back again, and their need for food and water was always satisfied miraculously. The Israelites also had clothing and shoes that never needed repair. They were able to travel day and night, based on Exodus 13:21-22 (NASB 2020): "And the Lord was going before them in a pillar of cloud by day to lead them on the way, and in a pillar of fire by night to give them light, so that they might travel by day and by night. He did not take away the pillar of cloud by day, nor the pillar of fire by night, from the presence of the people."

As Moses led the Israelites toward the Promised Land, it was inhabited by other nations who did not worship the Lord. God told Moses to send twelve spies to Canaan and evaluate their move forward to claim the land. Of the twelve spies, only two spies returned with a faith-filled report. The other ten described the land with fear, explaining that there were giants and danger, and it would be impossible for them to take the land. This resulted in an uproar among the people, as we can read in Numbers 14:2-4 (NASB 2020): "All the sons of Israel grumbled against Moses and Aaron; and the whole congregation said to them, 'Would that we had died in the land of Egypt! Or would that we had died in the wilderness!' So they said to one another, 'Let us appoint a leader and return to Egypt.'"

In Numbers 14:7-9 (NLT), Caleb and Joshua answered the crowd with their report! "They said to all the people of Israel, 'The land we traveled through and explored is wonderful! And if the Lord is pleased with us, he will bring us safely into that land and give it to us. It is a rich land flowing with milk and honey. Do not rebel against the Lord, and don't be afraid of the people of the land. They are only helpless prey to us! They have no protection, but the Lord is with us! Don't be afraid of them!" The Israelites would not hear it; this was also not the first time the Israelites had suggested such drastic measures, but this was certainly the most unreasonable time for them to do so. The Lord responded in Numbers 14:11, "How long will this people spurn Me? And how long will they not believe in Me, despite all the signs which I have performed in their midst?"

Without the leadership of God, Israel would never have left Egyptian bondage. After receiving the law at Mt. Sinai, these same people willingly affirmed, "All that the Lord has spoken we will do, and we will be obedient!" (Exodus 24:7b). Yet, they were in such a hurry to reject God's leadership that they decided to appoint a new leader and return to Egypt. They had a leader. God was their leader. They just didn't like where He was leading them. They were not trusting that He was faithful. Even in the midst of each aspect of faithfulness that they had depended on for their survival, they refused to continue to trust for the "Fullness of Time" to manifest. They were essentially saying, "We don't care what God promised us, we don't believe He can give it to us."

As a result of this lack of faith and disobedience, God declared, "Certainly all the people who have seen My glory and My signs which I performed in Egypt and the wilderness, yet have put Me to the test these ten times and have not listened to My voice, shall by no means see the land which I swore to their fathers, nor shall any of those who were disrespectful to Me see it" (Num 14:22–23). They heard the promise of God and saw His power to fulfill it, but they willingly rejected any hope of receiving that promise. Prior to Moses dying, Deuteronomy 34:4-5 says: "Then the Lord said to him, 'This is the land which I swore to Abraham, Isaac, and Jacob, saying 'I will give it to your descendants'; I have let you see it with your eyes, but you will not go over there.' So Moses, the servant of the Lord, died there in the land of Moab, in accordance with the word of the Lord." Although our God is a forgiving God, their lack of faith and their disobedience resulted in that generation never entering this land that had been promised to them. Joshua and Caleb, who walked in obedience, proclaiming faith when they first went as spies, were allowed to enter.

In Joshua 1:1-9, the Message Bible says, "Moses my servant is dead. Get going. Cross this Jordan River, you and all the people. Cross to the country I'm giving to the People of Israel. I'm giving you every square inch of the land you set your foot on—just as I promised Moses. From the wilderness and this Lebanon east to the Great River, the Euphrates River—all the Hittite country—and then west to the Great Sea. It's all yours. All your life, no one will be able to hold out against you. In the same way, I was with Moses, I'll be with you. I won't give up on you; I won't leave you. Strength! Courage! You are going to lead this people to inherit the land that I promised to give their ancestors. Give it everything you have, heart and soul. Make sure you carry out The Revelation that Moses commanded you, every bit of it. Don't get off track, either left or right, to ensure you get to where you're going. And don't let this Book of Revelation be out of mind for a minute. Ponder and meditate on it day and night, ensuring you practice everything written in it. Then you'll get where you're going; then you'll succeed. Haven't I commanded you? Strength! Courage! Don't be timid; don't get discouraged. God, your God is with you every step you take."

GOD'S FAITHFULNESS LEADS US TO KAIROS MOMENTS

As we walk in faith and obedience to God's revelation, we can believe that He is faithful! Remain in faith and obedience, for at the fullness of time, God will appear for you. God has made promises to you and every one of His people. God is no respecter of persons, and He can be trusted. What God has spoken with His mouth, His hand has the ability to perform!

What you have walked through thus far has been a time of preparation. We have seen examples in scripture: the time

Joseph spent between his home, Potiphar's house, the prison, and then with Pharoah. The years and years that Noah spent building the ark, preparing for a catastrophic event that the people had never seen. Esther prepared for her one day before the King, knowing what awaited her. Even the account of the lives of Shadrach, Meshach, and Abednego—preparing to be able to stand in the face of opposition, knowing that death was what the world promised if they continued to remain in faith. All of these demonstrations of faith and obedience also boiled down to the time that God was leading these mighty men and women of God in preparation and His faithfulness to do as He promised.

We are so accustomed to measuring time in the minutes, days, months, and years that our society depends on. Our finite and logical brain depends on our understanding of time. Remember that God can and does act completely outside of Chronos time. Our God is a Kairos God! As mentioned in Amos 9:13, things will happen so fast your head will spin! Joshua could have easily thrown his hands up in the air, reflecting on how much he had already walked through—the years in the desert for a short glimpse of the Promised Land and knowing what could be possible. Imagine if he had given up and not continued forward in obedience.

Joshua had a tight hold of the prophetic word that had been spoken for the children of Israel. He understood the call on his life and what God demanded of him. God had told him to be strong and courageous! He told Joshua to keep pressing on in boldness and faith and that he wouldn't leave Joshua's side! Joshua 11:15 says, "Just as God commanded his servant Moses, so Moses commanded Joshua, and Joshua did it. He didn't leave incomplete one thing that God had commanded Moses." Joshua could not dwell on disappointments and failures in the past; he also needed to continue walking forward without the guidance of his beloved teacher. He had walked through times of preparation, and now, Joshua was called to move forward into the critical strategic time where he could see God's promises come to fruition! God was providing him with an open door, and through obedience, God could lead Joshua and the children of Israel into a Kairos moment where the promise would be fulfilled in God's timeframe. They would no longer carry the weariness of the previous seasons and would see the blessing in the outcome of their obedience.

If you are in a season, walking in a season of preparation and believing for the fullness of time when you will see these promises come to pass, do not be discouraged. How often do we see Christians fall away when things get hard? How easy it is for us to say, "Let us appoint a leader and return to Egypt!" We are no different than Israel. Returning to sin means rejecting God's leadership. Returning to sin means rejecting God's promise. Returning to sin means rejecting our God-given freedom. May we never desire to "return to Egypt"! Instead, remember these verses in Philippians. "Not that I have already obtained all this, or have already arrived at my goal, but I press on to take hold of that for which Christ Jesus took hold of me. Brothers and sisters, I do not consider myself yet to have taken hold of it. But one thing I do: Forgetting what is behind and straining toward what is ahead, I press on toward the goal to win the prize for which God has called me heavenward in Christ Jesus." Philippians 3:12-14 (KJV).

I believe we are in a time when we see God's "sudden-lies" coming to pass, left and right, all around us. I encourage you to push forward toward your open door with determination and perseverance. Remember that regardless of how it appears around you, as you seek to hear direction from the Holy Spirit, watching and praying into what God is doing around you, you will see this fullness of time. Just like the last pieces placed in a jigsaw puzzle, God is completing the picture of what He has called you to. God has something for you right now, today, and in the future. A Kairos moment that brings you into a God moment!

"Yes indeed, it won't be long now." GOD's Decree. "Things are going to happen so fast your head will swim, one thing fast on the heels of the other. You won't be able to keep up. Everything will be happening at once— and everywhere you look, blessings! Blessings like wine pouring off the mountains and hills."

— Amos 9:13

CHAPTER 7

SUDDENLY MIRACLES

What are you believing for? Is it healing, deliverance, restoration, or a financial breakthrough? We know that God is not confined by time; He has worked many miracles that happened outside of our human understanding of possibilities! Kairos' moments are in His grasp, and we see people in scripture being healed and set free! Many accounts in the Bible of people believing in a move of God may be similar to what you have faith in today. The Bible shows us that there are times when God brought these miracles to pass instantly, changing the trajectory of the person's life.

We believe that through studying scripture, your faith can increase, and you will begin walking toward your sudden miracles. Romans 10:17 (NASB 2020) says, "So faith comes by hearing, and hearing by the word of Christ." Growing your faith can help your stance in believing for the suddenlies to come to pass.

Suddenly is often attributed to the words immediately,

instantly, swiftly, quickly. We see God accomplishing events much faster than what Chronos' time would allow or things happening that can only be explained by a move of God! I want to focus on several of these "suddenlies" from the word, knowing that what He has done before, He can do again.

Acts 10:34 (NASB 2020) says, "Then Peter replied, 'I see very clearly that God shows no favouritism. In every nation, he accepts those who fear him and do what is right.'" You can trust Him and trust His promises. It's going to happen! It's going to happen suddenly! As the omniscient, omnipresent Deity, God is not bound by the confines of space or time. "With the Lord, one day is as a thousand years and a thousand years as one day" 2 Peter 3:8b. We see in scripture God suddenly shows up on the scene. What God has promised, He can suddenly fulfill. It does not always take a long time to receive an incredible breakthrough.

BELIEVING FOR PROVISION

If you have found yourself in a position where you need help with your finances suddenly, there are "suddenly" miracles in the Bible that can help you increase your faith. These two women were on the verge of death, and suddenly, God stepped in, working through the obedience of His people, and completely shifted the situation.

God had commanded Elijah to stay in a specific place; Elijah would not need to be concerned for food or drink, for God would provide. All the bread Elijah would eat would be delivered by ravens in the morning and evening. Elijah was also able to drink water from the nearby brook. After a while, however, the brook dried up because there was no rain, so God told Elijah to go to Zarephath, and a widow would provide him with food. In 1 Kings 17, he saw a widow gathering sticks and asked her for water for him to drink. He also requested some bread. She answers him in verse 12 (NASB 2020): "But she said, 'As the Lord your God lives, I have no food, only a handful of flour in the bowl and a little oil in the jar; and behold, I am gathering a few sticks so that I may go in and prepare it for me and my son, so that we may eat it and die.' However, Elijah said to her, 'Do not fear; go, do as you have said. Just make me a little bread loaf from it first and bring it out to me, and afterwards, you may make one for yourself and for your son.'"

This woman had just enough food to allow her son and herself one more meal, and she had resolved for the two of them to die. Elijah was asking her to sacrifice the last of what she had, in essence, to sow seed for provision. In verse 14, Elijah continued: "For this is what the Lord, the God of Israel says; 'The bowl of flour shall not be used up, nor shall the jar of oil become empty until the day the Lord provides rain on the face of the earth.' So she went and did everything in accordance with the word of Elijah, and she and he and her household ate for many days. The bowl of flour was not used up, nor did the jar of oil become empty, in accordance with the word of the Lord, which He spoke through Elijah. When you believe God with the little that you have, He can suddenly turn it into an abundant harvest!

Like this widow in 2 Kings 4, we read of a woman in a similar situation, but God answers this prayer very differently. In the Message Bible, it says: "One day the wife of a man from the guild of prophets called out to Elisha, 'Your servant my husband is dead. You well know what a good man he was, devoted to God. And now the man to whom he was in debt is on his way to collect by taking my two children as slaves.' Elisha said, 'I wonder how I can be of help. Tell me, what do you have in your house?' 'Nothing,' she said. 'Well, I do have a little oil.' 'Here's what you do,' said Elisha. 'Go up and down the street and borrow jugs from all your neighbors. And not just a few, but everything you can get. Then come home and lock the door behind you and your sons. Pour oil into each container; when it each is full, set it aside.' She did what he said. She locked the door behind her and her sons; as they brought the containers to her, she filled them. When all the jugs and bowls were full, she said to one of her sons, 'Another jug, please.' He said, 'That's it. There are no more jugs.' That's when the oil stopped. She went and told the story to the man of God. He said, 'Go sell the oil and make good on your debts. Live, both you and your sons, on what's left.'"

Elisha provided this woman with specific instructions in preparing for her miracle. Borrowing jugs and bowls from her neighbors would have required an extent of the relationship with the people near her for her to be trusted with their possessions; therefore, this preparation process would have started before Elisha arrived with his guidance. As she and her sons poured the oil into each bowl and jug, they saw the miracle unfolding. The oil continued to flow until the last jug was full. Suddenly, it started, and suddenly, the supply was gone. They witnessed a "suddenly" miracle.

Both women were presented with an open door and a moment for opportunity. As they approached this open door, there was some required preparation: one was to prepare a cake for the prophet, and the other was to gather resources for her provision. The women were willing to be obedient—giving the last bit they had or going out to borrow treasured vessels from the people in the town. Each act was also a step of faith. God produced a "Kairos suddenly" in their lives and shifted their lives significantly where the fear they were facing was no longer an issue. Each example of preparation allowed for God to work in the fullness of time! Just as He did for the widows, He can turn your situation around in a Kairos moment!

BELIEVING FOR THE "GREATER THINGS"

Whether you are believing for a family member's salvation, or the Baptism of the Holy Spirit in your life, these can also happen as "suddenlies"! The baptism of the Holy Spirit and the ability to speak in tongues was a "suddenly" for the disciples in the book of Acts! In Acts 1:8, Jesus tells the disciples that they will receive power when the Holy Spirit comes upon them, helping them to be witnesses as they go out into the world. The disciples waited in Jerusalem for God's power, and "when the day of Pentecost fully came, they were all with one accord in one place suddenly there came a sound from heaven as of a rushing mighty wind, and it filled all the house where they were sitting" (Acts 2:1-2). It has been established that the move of the Holy Spirit in our lives is very dramatic, sudden, immediate, and instant. Although the baptism of the Holy Spirit and the ability to speak in tongues can appear suddenly in your life, it can also lead to suddenlies in other areas! Praying in tongues allows the believer to pray out the mysteries of God. It is communication between the believer and the Holy Spirit, to which adversaries have no access. God is giving us an avenue to bypass interference attempts from Satan and intercede for the open doors and suddenlies He is desiring to lead us to!

BELIEVING FOR HEALING

The Bible tells us in many verses of scripture that healing in the body is a promise from God. If you need a miracle in your body, I pray that these verses will help you build your faith and believe God for your "suddenly" miracle. In Luke 8 (NLT), he gives the account of the woman with the issue of blood. She had been dealing with this sickness and had spent all of her money trying to find a cure. With one encounter with Jesus, she received her healing. It was a Kairos moment! In verses 43-48, it says: "A woman in the crowd had suffered for twelve years with constant bleeding, and she could find no cure. Coming up behind Jesus, she touched the fringe of his robe. 'Who touched me?' Jesus asked. Everyone denied it, and Peter said, 'Master, this crowd is pressing against you.' But Jesus said, 'Someone deliberately touched me, for I felt healing power go out from me.' When the woman realized she could not stay hidden, she began to tremble and fell to her knees before him. The whole crowd heard her explain why she had touched him and that she had been immediately healed. 'Daughter,' he said to her, 'your faith has made you well. Go in peace.'"

This woman didn't just reach out to touch Jesus' robe. She

reached out and received it. It was her faith and expectancy, knowing that through Jesus she could receive, tugging on the anointing and healing her body miraculously and suddenly! When you are praying, believing for healing, pray with expectancy, trusting in God that you are receiving the things you are asking for. Remember, He is not a respecter of persons—the healing he has done for one person can also be done in your life!

We read in Mark 5 that Jairus, a local synagogue leader, told Jesus his daughter was very ill and needed prayer. Jesus was traveling to pray for her when he was stopped by the woman who touched His garment, desiring healing from the disease that had plagued her. While Jesus was speaking to the woman with the issue of blood, a messenger from Jairus' home approached him, saying that it was too late and his daughter had passed away. Jesus heard this exchange in Mark 5 and encouraged Jairus to not be afraid and to stand in faith. Jesus only allowed Peter, James, and John to accompany him into Jairus' home. When they went inside, there were many people there, weeping. Jesus assured the crowd that the little girl was not dead but just sleeping. Mark 5:40-42 in NLT says, "The crowd laughed at him. But he made them all leave, and he took the girl's father, mother, and three disciples into the room where the girl was lying. Holding her hand, he said to her, 'Talitha koum,' which means, 'Little girl, get up!' And the girl, who was twelve years old, immediately stood up and walked around! They were overwhelmed and amazed."

When Jairus approached Jesus, he was ready to believe for his daughter to be healed; when word came that she had passed away, he had a decision to make. In the Message

Bible, verse 35 says, "Your daughter is dead. Why bother the teacher anymore?" The natural thought was leading him to the belief that, ultimately, it was too late. They had missed their opportunity for her to be healed. Jesus was willing to give Jairus a "suddenly," with encouragement, Jairus followed obediently and in faith. Jesus performed a miracle when Jairus reached out to him in faith for his child. When the "suddenly" that you believe in comes to pass in your life, it can be life-changing for you! Nothing is impossible for God! Trust in Him, believe that He hears you, and hold onto the promise that you believe in.

Amos 9:13-15 from The Message Bible:

"Yes indeed, it won't be long now." GOD's Decree.

"Things are going to happen so fast your head will swim, one thing fast on the heels of the other. You won't be able to keep up. Everything will be happening at once—and everywhere you look, blessings! Blessings like wine pouring off the mountains and hills. I'll make everything right again for my people, Israel:

"They'll rebuild their ruined cities.

They'll plant vineyards and drink good wine.

They'll work in their gardens and eat fresh vegetables.

And I'll plant them, plant them on their land.

They'll never again be uprooted from the land I've given them."

GOD, your God, says so.

When God arises, sudden blessings unfold. The Bible gives examples of men and women believing in healing for themselves and their family members. A widow is reaching out hoping her prayers would be answered and she would have a miracle. It doesn't matter if Chronos time suggests that what you're believing for is impossible. We have seen multiple examples of how God can operate. He isn't bound by time! Kairos moments then and now allow us to glimpse the "other side." We peek around the corner at eternity. We actually get a glimpse of how God works. God desires for His people to be set free. He desires for His children to be healthy and whole, with nothing missing and nothing broken! We will see the transformation as we study His word, stand on His promises, and walk through the doors He holds open for us. Becoming more aware of what God is calling you to will lead to how you can work together with the Holy Spirit!

We are believing for the sudden arrival of the power of God! It can happen suddenly as we wait and expect to see God move. No matter how long or hard it has been, God has a "suddenly" for you: a sudden breakthrough. As we wait and trust God, we believe He will move; He will fulfill His promise, and we will receive from Him what we waited and looked for. Suddenly, health can change for the better, a total manifestation of healing just like the woman with the issue of blood. Suddenly, your finances will increase like the widow with Elisha. Suddenly, your loved one will be saved. Suddenly, God will move by His Spirit and fulfill His promises. Suddenly, everything will turn around. As God fulfilled His promises in the word, you will also see them come to pass in your life!

I believe that we are entering a time when followers of Christ establish the foundational pillars in their lives and their walk with Christ. As this occurs, you can walk in the fullness of preparation and time, resulting in seeing miracles happen. I am believing for the Body of Christ to start to walk out what Jesus tells the church to do in Mark 16:17-18 (NASB 2020), which says, "These signs will accompany those who have believed: in My name they will cast out demons, they will speak with new tongues; they will pick up serpents, and if they drink any deadly poison, it will not harm them; they will lay hands on the sick, and they will recover." We can follow the direction from God, taking our place that He has called us to, and as we see sudden miracles happening in our lives, we are also a testimony to who He is!

"All authority in heaven and on earth has been given to Me. Go, therefore, and make disciples of all the nations, baptizing them in the name of the Father and the Son and the Holy Spirit, teaching them to follow all that I commanded you; and behold, I am with you always, to the end of the age."

— MATTHEW 28:18B-20

CHAPTER 8

THE MANDATE

Believers can often get caught up in trying to discover God's call on their lives. Sometimes, this results in the person standing stagnant as they seek an answer or direction. They may not be very confident in the gifts or talents they see and may be unsure of the direction that God is leading them. God has a very important direction for all His children, a mandate to support expanding His kingdom and saving more people. The good news is that our God is a God of order, plans, and purposes. He has a plan and purpose for each person and desires to make that known.

The better news is that God clarifies that we can and expect to participate in this mission and provides everything we need. He calls us to do "greater things" than what Jesus accomplished while He was on earth. The time to act is now. Looking around at the world we live in, followers of Christ cannot afford to remain still, focusing only on the pieces we believe God to do in our lives. When the sons and daughters of God step into the call on their lives, they can walk in the fullness of His preparation and time. "Suddenlies" will come to pass, and we will witness testimonies of God operating outside of Chronos time. He desires to bless His people, to do miracles, signs, and wonders, and most of all, for people to come into a loving relationship with Him.

IN THE BEGINNING

In the beginning, God created everything, from the difference between night and day to the ocean's depths to the countless types of creatures that live on the earth. There was order, and there was a plan. God also communicated mandates to His people, directions, and results that He desired and planned for His people. A mandate is an official order or commission to do something. (Oxford Language Dictionary) Throughout the word, we see mandates that God is giving to His people. God gives us all the tools necessary to fulfill His mandate to His people, but it is up to us to seek His direction and wisdom to walk in this order.

God gave Adam and Eve specific instructions on what they should do. In essence, in the beginning, he issued them a mandate. Genesis 1:28 (MSG) says, "God blessed them: 'Prosper! Reproduce! Fill the earth! Take charge! Be responsible for fish in the sea and birds in the air, for every living thing that moves on the face of the earth." He told them, look—I want you to increase, multiply, subdue, and have dominion. I have given you this small piece; you can accomplish what I ask. I want you to grow what I've given you.

TIME TO OCCUPY

In Luke 19:11-13, Jesus tells His disciples about the parable of ten Minas. It says, "Now, while they were listening to these things, Jesus went on to tell a parable because He was near Jerusalem, and they thought that the kingdom of God was going to appear immediately. So He said, 'A nobleman went to a distant country to receive a kingdom for himself, and then return. And he called ten of his own slaves and gave them ten minas and said to them, 'Do business with this money until I come back.'"

Continuing to read in the parable, we can see that it was only when the servants presented an increase in what they had been given that the nobleman was pleased with their work. He had told them to occupy until He comes. As we discussed earlier in the book, the word "occupy" means to do business. The nobleman had given them the directions and the tools and trusted his servants to do as he asked. We know that Jesus came and dwelt among us. Before returning to Heaven, He communicated very clearly what we are to do—how we are to "occupy" until Christ's return.

This isn't something I created or invented. This came from God Himself. I get asked all the time, "What am I supposed to be doing?" I'm going to deliver to you a mandate, showing it to you directly from the word. I am referring to the mandate that Christ left his disciples. Now, you must ask yourself this question: am I a disciple? To answer that question, you need to understand what a disciple is.

Who is considered to be a disciple? A disciple is someone who is being taught. Eventually, you need to stop being taught and get to the point where you have "been taught." You need to reach the point where you accept that God trusts you with what He has provided. While you will continue to learn, you must take steps forward with the knowledge you already hold. This also simply answers the common question: what are we to do? Jesus is pointing out that He will do this to the end. Jesus gave his disciples a mandate. God paid the price through His son to equip you with everything you need to accomplish what He has asked. The ability and authority to fulfill this mandate are ours because of who Jesus is.

As the Christ and Lord, Jesus brought to pass the Old Testament prophecy to rule and reign forever and ever, which fulfilled the Davidic Covenant. Jesus was given the key of David to spiritually sit on David's throne and rule and reign over His people—and of His kingdom, there shall be no end. Isaiah 9:6 says, "For a child will be born to us, a Son will be given to us; and the government will rest on His shoulders; And His name will be called Wonderful Counselor, Mighty God, Eternal Father, Prince of Peace. In Revelation 3:7 it says that when Jesus was given the key of David, it indicated that all authority was given to Him. Those keys were a sign of authority. Jesus is the only One worthy to open the book sealed with seven seals. He is the Holy One, the True One, and the Faithful and True witness. He is the Authorized One. Revelation 1:18 says, "I am that liveth, and was dead; and, behold, I am alive always, Amen; and have the keys of Hell and of Death." (KJV)

What Jesus opens, no man can shut. Jesus also has the authority to shut doors, and what He shuts, no man can open. The key of David means that Jesus has authority no man possesses. The key of the house of David can also be understood as the power and authority to give access to God and eternal life. We know that Jesus is the Authorized One, giving us access to God and eternal life because the scripture says, "For there is one God, and one mediator between God and men, the man Christ Jesus" 1 Tim 2:5 (NASB 2020)

IT'S TIME TO GO!

Just like he told all His disciples, we are charged to "go"! Matthew 28:16-20 NASB 2020: "But the eleven disciples proceeded to Galilee, to the mountain which Jesus had designated. And when they saw Him, they worshipped Him, but some were doubtful. And Jesus spoke to them, saying, "All authority in heaven and on earth has been given to Me. Go, therefore, and make disciples of all the nations, baptizing them in the name of the Father and the Son and the Holy Spirit, teaching them to follow all that I commanded you; and behold, I am with you always, to the end of the age." The wording of the verse specifies "the end of the age." In the New King James translation, the wording is "even unto the end of the world." God never intended for the Great Commission to end with the disciples. Some people believe this mandate ended or that the power to complete the mandate was no longer present. These ideas are simply not accurate. The mandate was to continue, just as the word said His presence would.

In Acts 10:38 (NASB 2020), the Bible says, "You know of Jesus of Nazareth, how God anointed Him with the Holy Spirit and with power, and how He went about doing good and healing all who were oppressed by the devil, for God was with Him." Verses 42-43 continue: "And He ordered us to preach to the people and to testify solemnly that this is the One who has been appointed by God as a Judge of the living and the dead. All the prophets testify of Him, that everyone who believes in Him receives forgiveness of sins through His name." Through His son, God paid the price and made way for us, though we were once sinners, so that we can have eternity with Him in heaven. God desires that ALL would come into a relationship with Him. This is why it is so important that we accept this assignment and move forward. He said this is what I want you to do. We need to get into the practice of desiring all that is available to us because of Jesus' sacrifice—and this mandate is no different.

BEING A WITNESS

These verses still apply today; some have the power of the Holy Spirit but choose not to be witnesses. It is easy to believe that the main responsibility of being a witness would fall on the members of the Five-Fold Ministry: the Apostle, the prophet, the Evangelist, the Pastor, and the Teacher. No—YOU are mandated. In reality, this mandate applies to all born-again believers. Jesus Christ went about doing good. To be like Jesus, that is what we need to do. We need to go about doing good. Every believer can and should be a witness for Jesus. The first word in the sentence on the Great Commission is Go! Acts 1:8 (NLT) says, "But you will receive power when the Holy Spirit has come upon you, and you will be my witnesses in Jerusalem, in all Judea and Samaria, and to the ends of the earth." Go to your neighbor, go to work, go to the streets, and while you are at each place, you must be a witness. In those places, go about doing good. As we live this lifestyle, striving for the day when we can hear God say, "Well done, my good and faithful servant" (Matthew 25:21). Realistically, the first indication of this being a possibility for you is that other people around you will be hearing God's words flowing out of your mouth. Your thoughts and words align with His, and your life follows suit. The way you live is a walking testimony for whom you serve.

In his book, *"Why Revival Tarries,"* Leonard Ravenhill tells a story about a criminal named Charlie Peace who was a serial murderer. "As Charlie walked to the gallows, the chaplain read from *"The Consolations of Religion."* The text covers Bible verses about hell. Charlie was amazed that the chaplain was reading the passages without much emotion rather than trying to convert Charlie. After all, this would be Charlie's last chance at salvation. These were his last moments of life before being killed and going to eternity. As he read, the chaplain described hell as a pit with no bottom and an eternal fire that does not consume. The chaplain had zero emotion reading this document. It was as if the chaplain didn't even believe what he was reading; his voice had no unction. Charlie said the following to the chaplain: 'Sir,' addressing the preacher, 'If I believed what you and the church of God say that you believe, even if England were covered with broken glass from coast to coast, I would walk over it, if need be, on hands and knees and think it worthwhile living, just to save one soul from an eternal hell, separated from a loving God!'"(Ravenhill, 2004) Ravenhill summarizes the source of the problem—with both the chaplain and the present-day church, as the loss of the Holy Spirit in the church—a concern even in 1959 when Ravenhill wrote the first edition of his book. He said that the very catalyst that makes us witnesses has been removed from the body of Christ.

How do we know that the Great Commission is not happening? Barna Research tackled this question in 2018 and their study on the Great Commission in America had scary findings. Fifty percent of churchgoers do not even know what the Great Commission is. Another six percent are not sure about the commission. The bottom line is that seventeen percent understand the meaning of the Great Commission. If people barely make it to the church building, how would it be an expectation that they would go out and be witnesses as the Great Commission mandates us to do? Millennials, who compose the largest unchurched group, have the worst numbers of people who understand the commission. The results came back with this group at ten percent. Every generation below us that is not raised up, is losing information. The mandate of the Great Commission is being lost as time goes on. Considering the effect on the youngest generation, we have seen prayer and recognition of the power of the Holy Spirit leaving the church itself. As it left the church, it was also less recognized in schools. (Barna Research, 2018, March 27)

Considering the trend of the statistics from Barna Research, we have a Biblical account of what can happen if younger generations are not taught about the truth of God. The sobering realization of how vital it is for Christians to take this mandate as a personal mission and go out to make disciples. In Judges 2, we read that Joshua had just died and was buried. The Message Bible says: "Eventually, that entire generation died and was buried. Then, another generation grew up and didn't know anything about God or the work He had done for Israel. The people of Israel did evil in God's sight: They served Baal-gods; they deserted God, the God of their parents who had led them out of Egypt; they took up with other gods, gods of the peoples around them. And oh, how they angered God. (Judges 2:10-12) Thankfully, we are not alone in this mandate, and the Holy Spirit desires to lead us moving forward to change the reality we are currently seeing.

The Holy Spirit is essential in being a witness for Christ. When I was baptized in the Holy Spirit, I no longer had to "try" or "work" to be born again. Before that, it was a struggle! The Holy Spirit became a restrainer in my life. With the Holy Spirit, I don't need to try to love you. I can't help but love you. The Holy Spirit makes you a witness because He is working to transform your life. Sometimes, we think we can fall back on qualities we have based on how we were raised or our genes. Our personality traits. Christ overrides every bad gene in your life. He can break every generational curse or every spirit you carried in your hereditary background. His blood is better than that. He cleanses from ALL unrighteousness. (1 John 1:9) You are no longer who you were; you are born again with the Holy Spirit leading you. He makes you a witness, telling you to go and be a good example.

We know from scripture that before the Holy Spirit dwelled in Peter, he denied Jesus three times! Following receiving the Holy Spirit, Peter witnessed thousands of people being saved as he served as a witness! He went from being the "Coward of Calvary" to the "Preacher of Pentecost." Peter transitioned from hiding and denying to standing and preaching. One thing happened. He got filled with the Holy Spirit. The ingredient we need to continue carrying the mandate Jesus gave us is the Baptism of the Holy Spirit. You don't need a class to learn how to be a witness. You need the person of the Holy Spirit to fill you up and baptize you. When the disciples came out of the upper room and got down to the bottom of the steps, they had a language that crossed barriers. It crossed languages, connecting with people from different backgrounds, ethnicities, and even broke down prejudice. They suddenly had a language to communicate. They could move forward, doing exactly as God directed in the book of Matthew. We know from the Book of Acts that the number of followers increased exponentially then. Putting it simply, they became witnesses with the baptism of the Holy Spirit.

In Genesis, God told Adam and Eve that He wanted them to increase, multiply, subdue, and have dominion. When Jesus was telling the parable of the ten minas, He said that the nobleman had ordered the people to occupy, to continue with business. He wasn't telling them to maintain; he was desiring an increase! In verses in Matthew, when Jesus is giving the Great Commission, He is telling the disciples to go into all the nations, teaching as we have been taught and adding to the number.

It is time, church. When asked, Pastor Rod Parsley, my pastor, has a great answer about why we are here. His response, which is also an order at the same time, is that we are here because they are not. We have empty seats in the church, both literally and figuratively, because there are still people out there who have yet to know who God is. Some people are hurting and desperate to come into a loving relationship with their savior. The problem is they don't know exactly what that looks like, assuming the accuracy of the worldview that they have come to know. We hold the answer to the question they may not know how to ask. There is a ministry that must continue to move forward for each of us individually and also as a whole. It is time for us as the church—the ecclesia—to rise, realize what is at stake, and follow God's mandate.

"So here's what I want you to do, God helping you: take your ordinary life—your sleeping, eating, going-to-work, and walking-around life and place it before God as an offering, Embracing what God does for you is the best thing you can do for Him"

— Romans 12:1 (msg)

CHAPTER 9

THE MINISTRY

The church is shifting to a kingdom culture. When I say kingdom, it's not about me. It is about showing Christ to everyone you come in contact with. Every one of you are called to the ministry. The word ministry is the spiritual work or service of any Christian. You are called somewhere to someone, period. You need to decide today to allow Christ to use you, not necessarily on a platform or with a microphone, but in your life and circle!

Ministry will never look exactly the same for any two people. There are certain people that only you can reach. Your pastor will not have access to the same people as you. You need to appreciate the role God has given you in the body! As we are familiar with the mandate to which God called the body of believers, we all have a specific part to play. Some people never set foot in a church. Others grew up in church, but due to what is now commonly known as "church hurt," they vow never to return. Through all that, our God is loving and merciful and still desires for those people to enter into a relationship with Him.

When I was a boy, we showed up and watched the church, but nobody told me I had to "be" the church. From what I could tell, it was basically a spectator sport. Similar churches are still operating today, raising up "sheeple"—people who are watchers or consumers and are just sitting in Tabernacles across America, but they're not doing anything with what they're getting. Going to church on a Sunday morning is not about punching your time card or checking a box when you're done for the week. We need to take what we've been given, what we're here for today, and we need to take it to the world around us.

People learn about God's love for them by how much, or how well, the church functions in the world. Your neighbor needs you to be Christ to them. If you have a "Jesus" sticker on the back of your car, your driving should match who you say you are. The world around us needs us to take up the mandate and the ministry. Every Christian has a role and responsibility. We all have a circle of influence that is specific only to us.

PARTS OF THE BODY

1 Corinthians 12:12-22 (NLT) says, "The human body has many parts, but the many parts make up one whole body. So it is with the body of Christ. Some of us are Jews, some are Gentiles, some are slaves, and some are free. But we have all been baptized into one body by one spirit and share the same spirit. Yes, the body has many different parts, not just one part. If the foot says, 'I am not part of the body because I am

not a hand,' that does not make it any less a part of the body. And if the ear says, 'I am not part of the body because I am not an eye,' would that make it any less a part of the body? If the whole body were an eye, how would you hear? Or if your whole body were an ear, how would you smell anything? But our bodies have many parts, and God has put each part just where he wants it. How strange a body would be if it had only one part! Yes, there are many parts, but only one body. The eye can never say to the hand, 'I don't need you.' The head can't say to the feet, 'I don't need you.' Some body parts that seem weakest and least important are the most necessary.

We must develop this mindset in the body of Christ. The church is God's hands, feet, and voice, and people primarily learn about God's love for them by what they see from us and how it matches what we say. As previously mentioned, the responsibility of fulfilling the Great Commission is not limited to the apostle, the prophet, the evangelist, the pastor, and the teacher; the members of the fivefold ministry have an added responsibility. They also work to equip us to go out into the world. Ephesians 4:12-13 (AMPC) "His intention was the perfecting *and* the full equipping of the saints (His consecrated people), [that they should do] the work of ministering toward building up Christ's body (the church), [That it might develop] until we all attain oneness in the faith and in the comprehension of the [full and accurate] knowledge of the Son of God, that [we might arrive] at really mature manhood (the completeness of personality which is nothing less than the standard height of Christ's own perfection), the measure of the stature of the fullness of the Christ *and* the completeness found in Him."

I love the Message Bible's language for the next three verses: "No prolonged infancies among us, please. We'll not tolerate babes in the woods, small children who are easy prey for predators. God wants us to grow up, to know the whole truth and tell it in love-like Christ in everything. We take our lead from Christ, who is the source of everything we do. He keeps us in step with each other. His very breath and blood flow through us, nourishing us so that we will grow up healthy in God, robust in love." (Ephesians 4:14-16 MSG)

IT IS YOUR TURN

I'm talking about everyone sitting in a pew, week after week. You need to know today that God is tagging you in. These verses in Ephesians 4 describe what we are getting equipped to do. The goal of attending church every Sunday is not to try harder to live right or to have a better life. When you arrive to have communion with the body of believers, pray for your heart to be prepared for service equipping. To prepare to go out into your ministry.

If this world is ever going to transform, it will be because you take the ministry of Jesus into this world. The Great Commission in Matthew 28:19-20 commands us to make disciples—not just converts. This allows members of the body to go out, witnessing and inviting unbelievers to believe in Jesus for eternal life and then for them to follow Jesus in this life. Ephesians 4 describes the equipping of the saints, the church members are made disciples. You are that disciple, equipped and inviting.

2 CORINTHIANS 5:16-20 (MSG)

[16-20]Because of this decision, we don't evaluate people by what they have or how they look. We looked at the Messiah that way once and got it all wrong, as you know. We certainly don't look at him that way anymore. Now we look inside and see that anyone united with the Messiah gets a fresh start and is created new. The old life is gone; a new life emerges! Look at it! All this comes from God, who settled the relationship between us and him and then called us to settle our relationships with each other. God put the world square with himself through the Messiah, giving the world a fresh start by offering forgiveness of sins. God has given us the task of telling everyone what he is doing. We're Christ's representatives. God uses us to persuade men and women to drop their differences and enter into God's work of making things right between them. We're speaking for Christ himself now: Become friends with God; he's already a friend with you.

It may not always be convenient if we are committed to ministering where God opens doors and leads us to speak, love on, or pray for people. You may have gone into Walmart with a specific mission or plan—to run in, find the items you're looking for, and get out as quickly as possible. God often takes these opportunities to open our eyes and show us the people He desires for us to minister to! The person He leads us to may not look like we do, smell like we are used to, or may have gone through a different hell than we've experienced. Even if we don't feel ready or equipped, it isn't based on our ability but on our availability. We need to make sure that we see the people around us with the eyes of Christ, love them as He does, and desire for that person to come into a loving relationship with our savior. It may start with something as simple as letting the person know that God loves them. He will always give you what you need in the moment.

YOUR ORDINARY LIFE

Where do we, the body, start in ministry? Romans 12:1-2 in the Message Bible says: "So here's what I want you to do, God helping you: take your ordinary life—your sleeping, eating, going-to-work, and walking-around life and place it before God as an offering, Embracing what God does for you is the best thing you can do for Him. Don't become so well-adjusted to your culture that you fit into it without even thinking. Instead, fix your attention on God. You'll be changed from the inside out. Readily recognize what he wants from you and quickly respond to it. Unlike the culture around you, always dragging you down to its level of immaturity, God brings the best out of you and develops well-formed maturity in you."

These verses are breaking down each portion of our day-to-day life. Our life at home, our professional life, our relaxation or leisure time. Each part of our life is to be offered to Him, looking for opportunities to serve. Just as Ravenhill described in his book—if we have a true revelation of what God is calling us to, how profound of a truth that has been revealed to us, we would have such a deep passion for sharing the truth of His love with anyone and everyone. How desperate are you to tell people about who Jesus is? Everywhere you go, you are a billboard. Everywhere you go, somebody's looking at your life and thinking either "I need what they got," or worse, "No thanks, I'm out." "Spiritual work or service" in your life will fit you and the gifts He gave you. The goal is to be mindful of the ministry God has called you to and what Romans 12:1 looks like for you.

Several years ago, I was working for a large corporation, and when they hired me, they told me I couldn't talk about Jesus unless someone inquired, and I couldn't hand out tracks. I told them that was fine and went to do my work. Someone was leaving tracks in the bathroom at one point, and I was confronted about it. When I assured them that I was aware of the rule and it was not me doing that, they said they thought I was the only Christian there.

Our ministry is not to be limited to slipping tracks on the table in stealth mode without any ownership of the truth we're communicating. The way we act, speak, and carry ourselves (even our countenance) must be consistent with the God we say we serve. Also, we must work with excellence, as Colossians 3:23-24 (NASB 2020) reminds us: Whatever you do, do your work heartily, as for the Lord and not for people, knowing that it is from the Lord that you will receive the reward of the inheritance. It is the Lord Christ whom you serve." Many times, I have desired to work with excellence that God has used to open a door in ministry to people around me.

The company I worked for brought people in from Japan to train the employees. We had no real language communication, so they could only understand my expression. I made it my practice to show up early for work every morning, on my line and doing my job. Like I said, I did my work with excellence. When they saw me, I was waving and smiling. I greeted them, telling them good morning. One morning, in broken English, one man asked me why I was always so happy. It allowed me to tell him exactly where my joy came from: Jesus Christ lives in me. Through the pendent he wore, he was able to show me what his god looked like.

Through this very limited conversation, he realized that he needed to know my God. I developed relationships with several of the people I worked with. I loved them, and they knew I loved them. Eventually, they came to church with me. They ended up getting saved. From that one moment, suddenly, we had entered the fullness of time where faithfulness to excellence and showing the love of Jesus led to the fulfillment of the mandate. Ministry is showing the love of Christ. If you are lost and you see someone with an outward expression of love, joy, peace, happiness, and wholeness, you want to be with that person. You want what they have. It is up to us to live a life that exemplifies the Christ who lives in us and our hope in Him. How we present ourselves should point to who we are in Christ. This is our ministry. I take my ordinary life daily and lay it on the altar.

Colossians 4:2-6 (NASB 2020) says, "Devote yourselves to prayer, keeping alert in it with an attitude of thanksgiving; praying at the same time for us as well, that God will open up to us a door for the word so that we may proclaim the mystery of Christ, for which I have also been imprisoned That I may make it clear in the way I ought to proclaim it.

Conduct yourselves with wisdom toward outsiders, making the most of every opportunity. Your speech must always be with grace, as though seasoned with salt, so that you will know how you should respond to each person." While in prison, Paul sought God, praying for open doors and divine opportunities to share the gospel with others. He was praying to be ready at all times, with the desire for souls always as his top priority. Your ministry can infiltrate every aspect of your life if you allow it.

When you go out with friends, would you ever be willing to pray for your server if the Holy Spirit speaks a need to you? Would the people you are with take it in stride or be in a state of shock? The sad truth is that many Christians do not act Christ-like when they are out, including eating in restaurants. My mama was a waitress for 30 years at the same place. She used to say the worst day to work is Sunday. She said, I don't like working Sundays because that's when all the Christians show up after their church service lets out.

Most servers will say that the Sunday morning crowds are usually rude and less generous than the people there on other days during the week. Imagine if there could be a spark of God's mandate for Christians, allowing our everyday life to focus more on winning souls and less on our personal agenda. I just picture a shift where we are known for our love. Christians extending the love and grace that has been offered to them. Demonstrating the character of Christ can change the trajectory of someone's life. Ephesians 5:16 AMP: "Making the very most of your time [on earth, recognizing and taking advantage of each opportunity and using it with wisdom and diligence], because the days are [filled with] evil.

We are all called, equipped, and qualified to live a life that glorifies God. As you walk in a Romans 12:1 mindset, people around you will know you by your fruit. People will desire to be around you and will want to know the "how" and "why." How are you so content when there is trouble around you? How are you always so full of joy? Why do you tip well when you go to restaurants and ask your server if there's anything they need prayer for? Many times, when people see you walking these verses out in your life, it will spark their curiosity, and you have opportunities to share exactly who Jesus is.

Your ministry needs to infiltrate every aspect of your life. It is not like your career where you clock in and clock out, and you have weekends off and holidays. When you are at the grocery store, taking your dog for a walk, or at the park with your children, God can bring someone into your vision who may need encouragement, a smile, or even intercession for healing. Your ministry doesn't need to hand you a microphone to speak in front of hundreds of people. We know from the word that our life is but a vapor (James 4:14). We have very limited time to take up the torch Jesus left when He was here on earth and carry it—doing our part to fulfill the Great Commission.

We have opportunities to reach people that only we can speak to. We must make ourselves available, listening for His voice so that He might lead us and open doors to whom we can minister. God desires to continue to grow and develop His children so they can walk in the call and the plan He has for their lives. Look for the people you can learn from and also the people you can help guide as we continue to be the hands and feet of Christ.

Do not conform to the pattern of this world,

but be transformed by renewing your mind.

Then, you can test and approve what God's

will is—his good, pleasing, and perfect will.

— Romans 12:2 (NIV)

CHAPTER 10

THE MANTLE

JEREMIAH 29:11 NASB

"For I know the plans that I have for you, 'declares the Lord, 'Plans for prosperity and not for disaster, to give you a future and a hope." (NASB 2020)

God has something amazing for you. It is full of future and hope, just as the Bible tells us. Something that is specifically designed for you, fitted for you. God has a mantle for your life, or another way to think of it is a destiny for your life. A mantle is a scriptural metaphor or symbol for a calling, ministry, anointing, and (when applicable) an office given to individuals by God. The area that He is calling you to is something that you're passionate about. If I can talk you out of it, then you're not called to it. You need to get to the vein that you're called to. It's like you have a lane to yourself, going down the road. The highway is wide open ahead of you, ready for you to walk in your calling!

THE CHARACTER REQUIRED

Many of us are looking for promotion before we're looking for the character to carry the promotion. Understand your calling will be tested over time. God is not questioning the call. He's questioning the character. God positions you with people and leaders that he wants you to serve. Now, serving with faithfulness and a teachable heart is a powerful means of being positioned to attain your God-ordained destiny. Years ago, I was serving under my pastor. We would fly around the United States, and I served by running the book and media table for him. At the same time, I pastored a church that was seating a thousand, and I was working a book table. I was serving, gleaning, and growing. There comes a point where God's no longer trying to connect you to the man of God. You've done that. Now he's trying to connect you to your call.

One day, when I was serving, it was raining. We used to wear suits and ties all the time. So I had on a pair of shoes, probably almost a thousand dollars, on a suit that was about $2,800. I remember standing outside in the rain under an awning that was not working very well, working a book table. They had a Jumbo Tron screen out on the football field because the building was packed. They had service for three hours, and no one came and got me. Man of God, a faith and power pastor in the church, and here I was out on the sidewalk. I went through the whole service. I never sat down. The service ended, and they came and picked up the blue bag for the bank. The guy came and got it, thanked me, and directed me to pack everything back up to send back to Ohio.

I didn't get to leave the table until I got everything packed away. So there I was, and I needed to go to the restroom. Walking down the hall, I thought, "Who does he think he is? I ain't never setting up another dadgum book table." As I was washing my hands, I threw the towel, and it missed the trash can. It missed and hit the floor after bouncing one time. I thought, "Somebody will get that." I turned to reach for the door to go out of the bathroom, and when I did, the Holy Spirit set down on me. At that moment, I crumpled up on the floor. I crawled around on that floor, tears running down my face. God said you're not ready for your next mantle. I cleaned that whole bathroom that day. I cleaned the walls. I didn't have cleaning stuff. I had brown paper towels and water. I cleaned. I cleaned everything. All of it: the toilet, the outside, the floor. When I got done, I had big brown stains on that $2,800 suit, and all my shoes were scuffed up.

When God is leading through the time I've referred to as "fullness of preparation," pruning must take place. You must be willing to let go of the old, going through a place of separation. Having a true encounter with God and being transformed by the Holy Spirit will allow you to be used for His glory. Proverbs 25:4-5 in the Message says, "Remove impurities from the silver, and the silversmith can craft a fine chalice; remove the wicked from leadership and authority will be credible and God-honoring. I had to surrender to the Holy Spirit, allowing Him to identify and remove the remaining pieces between us. Romans 12:2 (NIV) says, "Do not conform to the pattern of this world but be transformed by the renewing of your mind. Then you will be able to test and approve what God's will is — his good, pleasing, and perfect will." This season of preparation is developing you to carry the mantle and the calling that is on your life.

You cannot move forward and stay still at the same time. If you want to move into the greater things God has for you, you must be willing to separate yourself from things that could be holding you back. Romans 12:9b says, "Hate what is evil; cling to what is good." Next, you have to go through a place of transformation. God can only work with the things you're willing to give Him. If you spend too much time trying to hide the things you're ashamed of or deny your shortcomings, you'll miss your opportunity to be transformed and move on from who you used to be into who God created you to be. You must do more than go to church Sunday after Sunday.

MENTORSHIP

Throughout scripture, we see that God calls people (both men and women) into relationships with someone who may be seen as a mentor. You may pursue this relationship when someone exemplifies a quality that you are having difficulty with or want to develop further; the mentor can guide you in growth in that area. Also seen in the church, this can occur when people have a similar calling on their lives, and God establishes a relationship through honor and obedience. This relationship would enable you to walk alongside this other person, learning and gleaning from everything they have walked through in their own relationship with the Lord. The mentee is often able to gain wisdom from difficulties and pitfalls that their mentor has experienced but can also serve as a support for their teacher as they continue forward together.

It is through this relationship that God can call for a mantle to be passed from one to the next, just as we see in scripture.

MOSES AND JOSHUA

Joshua walked alongside Moses for approximately forty years. While he did not experience everything to the same extent as Moses, God was able to use this time and wisdom to prepare Joshua for what he would face for the rest of his life. Joshua accompanied Moses on Mt. Sinai in Exodus 24:13-18. Joshua remained as Moses continued to the top, where he met with God. In Exodus 32, Joshua was with Moses when they descended from Mt. Sinai and found the Israelites in the middle of their idolatry, dancing before the golden calf. Joshua witnessed as Moses threw the tablets down to the ground. Joshua witnessed many miracles of God through Moses. In Deuteronomy 34:9, Moses had just died. The Message Bible mentions a mantle being passed to Joshua: "Joshua son of nun was filled with the spirit of wisdom because Moses had laid his hands on him. The People of Israel listened obediently to him and did the same as when God had commanded Moses." God then warns Joshua on how to continue on after the death of his beloved teacher. God still had great plans for Joshua, and God expected him to continue carrying the mantle to lead his people through the time of the manifestation of His promise. God would use Joshua to lead His people into the Promised Land, which would only happen in His fullness of time.

God may develop a "Moses" relationship in your life, teaching and maturing aspects of the mantle God has for you and also the ministry that you are walking in. God positions you with people that He wants you to serve. There is something about that person's mantle that God wants you to glean from. So much of this teaching comes down to your character and the need to prune what cannot remain.

ELIJAH AND ELISHA

The relationship between Elijah and Elisha in the Bible is an excellent example of a mantle being passed from one person to the next. In reference to Elisha's passion, there were many times in 2 Kings that Elijah told Elisha to go home, but he refused. Through the prophecy given to Elijah and the prophetic act, God's plan was set in motion.

> 1 KINGS 19:15-16 (NASB 2020)
>
> The Lord said to him, "Go, return on your way to the wilderness of Damascus; and when you have arrived, you shall anoint Hazael king over Aram. You shall also anoint Jehu, the son of Nimshi, king over Israel, and you shall anoint Elisha, the son of Shaphat of Abel-Jehovah, as a prophet in your place.

God was telling Elijah, "I am going to lead you to a place, and you will meet someone there. You're going to anoint that man, and I have a plan for him." Again, this is not just a case of being in the right place at the right time. Elisha needed to cooperate with the call of God—but he did not choose the call of God. He had to follow the call to receive the mantle that was his by God's appointment. You don't just drop everything you have just on a whim. Elisha dropped every-thing. His hunger and pursuit of Elijah were a sign of what God had placed in his heart. God calls. God chooses.

1 KINGS 19:19-21 (NASB 2020)

So he departed from there and found Elisha the son of Shaphat while he was plowing, with twelve yoke of oxen in front of him, and he with the twelfth. And Elijah came over to him and threw his cloak on him. Then he left the oxen behind and ran after Elijah and said, "Please let me kiss my father and my mother, then I will follow you." And he said to him, "Go back, for what have I done to you?" So he returned from fol-lowing him and took the pair of oxen and sacrificed them, and cooked their meat with the implements of the oxen, and gave it to the people, and they ate. Then he got up and followed Elijah and served him.

Elisha made a decision to leave everything behind! God places a desire in our hearts that moves us toward our destiny; He uses prophecy, His Word, mentors, the body of Christ, the Holy Spirit, and many other things to move us toward the specific calling that is ours. During this season, God was also using Elijah to recognize, prepare, and establish the appoint-ment. If you are looking to receive the mantle for your life, you will need to look for the passion to serve and honor the leaders and the call that He has placed in your heart. God has established His timeline for your life that develops your character and your heart. God positions you with people and leaders that he wants you to serve in your walk toward your destiny. God uses those in leadership and authority over us to recognize and establish us in that calling at the right time. Serving with faithfulness and a teachable heart is a powerful means of being positioned to attain your God-ordained destiny. What you are mantled for will come to pass. During this season in your life, you must serve, trust, and honor!

In 2 Kings 2:9, Elijah asks Elisha what he can do for Elisha before he is taken up, to which Elisha requests a double portion of Elijah's spirit. Elijah responds in 2 Kings 2:10 (NASB 2020): He said, "You have asked a hard thing. Nevertheless, if you see me when I am taken from you, it shall be so for you; but if not, it shall not be so." You can't give someone double of what you have. At least a portion of this transaction would need to be between Elisha's heart and God's. The delivery of the double portion was directly tied to the intensity of his focus on the assignment.

The time was coming quickly for Elijah to leave and for the mantle to be passed to Elisha. This would definitely be an example of a Kairos moment—a portion of time that cannot be measured with our human mind! There was a shift that was coming, and instead of Elisha lagging behind, struggling to keep up with his leader, Elisha was determined to not only lay hold of everything that Elijah had—but he had his mind and heart set on even more! In the kingdom, you are not just the product of your environment—you are a product of your pursuit as well. If you weren't born with it, you need to fight, serve, and believe in it. Ultimately, you must determine to never quit!

Elisha did see Elijah leave in a chariot of fire. He then tore his own garment in two pieces, and in 2 Kings 2:13

NASB, it says, "He also took up the coat of Elijah that had fallen from him, and he went back and stood by the bank of the Jordan. Then he took Elijah's coat that had fallen from him and struck the waters and said, 'Where is the Lord, the God of Elijah?' And when he also had struck the waters, they were divided here and there, and Elisha crossed over. Now, when the sons of the prophets who were at Jericho opposite him saw him, they said, 'The spirit of Elijah has settled on Elisha.' And they came to meet him and bowed down to the ground before him." (NASB 2020)

Elisha was a servant to Elijah. He supported him in a menial way and learned at his feet. In 2 Kings 3:11, we see Elisha's previous season prophesying his next." But Jehoshaphat said, 'Is there no prophet of the Lord here, that we may inquire of the Lord by him?' And one of the king of Israel's servants answered and said, 'Elisha the son of Shaphat is here, who used to pour water on the hands of Elijah.'" (NASB 2020) After this transfer, he took up the work of his spiritual father and operated in the office of the prophet. The Bible records twice as many miracles for Elisha as were recorded under Elijah's ministry —with one exception, raising someone from the dead; however, death didn't even stop God from the miraculous. In 2 Kings 13:20-21, the Message Bible says: "Then Elisha died and they buried him. Sometime later, raiding bands of Moabites, as they often did, invaded the country. One day, some men were burying a man and spotted the raiders. They threw the man into Elisha's tomb and got away. When the body touched Elisha's bones, the man came alive, stood up, and walked out on his own two feet." (MSG) Elisha's prayer and God's promise for a double portion were not even stopped by death! The promise for the double portion resulted in works even beyond death!

It is possible that you will wear a series of mantles. Before he took up Elijah's mantle, Elisha was first a worker in his father's field, and then he wore the garb of a servant. Your next promotion may not look any different compared to where you are right now; the only differences may be where you're doing it and the heart you're doing it with. Understand that you're still going to serve. When God took Elijah, Elisha took his own cloak. The Bible said that he had worn it and ripped it in two. He made a decision that day. I'm not going back to where I was. I'm going to take off last season's mantle, and I'm going to pick up this next season's mantle.

JOSEPH

Joseph had a series of physical mantles on his life. He had a coat of many colors; after that, Potiphar gave him a cloak as the head slave master. He then ran the whole prison. In Genesis 41:42, Pharaoh rolled him in his garments that represented his position as ruler next to Pharaoh. "Pharaoh took off his signet ring, put it on Joseph's hand, clothed him in garments of fine linen, and put a gold necklace around his neck." (NASB 2020) This transition did not happen overnight, and in no way was it automatic. Joseph had to serve in every single season; he served even when people were accusing him, and he had done nothing wrong. Joseph stayed in obedience, growing and developing his character, and knew that God would lead him to a place of victory!

FORWARD MOMENTUM

Your character continues to develop as he prunes and burns away portions that are not of Him. This process is not typically easy or short-term and depends on our willingness to be humble in the work He desires to do. As you seek God for this development and maturing, He is faithful. "Ask, and it will be given to you; seek, and you will find; knock and the door will be opened to you." (Matthew 7:7). The transformation that He desires to do in your life allows you to walk in the ministry that He has planned for you! As God continues to develop the character of His children through guidance directly from the Holy Spirit or from one in life as a mentor, the ability and willingness to serve should remain in the heart.

There are some moves that God is willing to do, but He is waiting on us. God is saying, if I can get the right character here, I can take you to this place. The next promotion in your life is based on where you are now and not where you want to be. How you serve now will determine where you're going next. Acts 6:6 (NASB 2020): "And they brought these men before the apostles; and after praying, they laid their hands on them." These men didn't get promoted on their own. They submitted themselves to instruction by those whom God had placed in a position in their lives. We don't self-mantle our ministries. God uses those in authority around us to recognize and establish us in the calling at the right time.

As Joshua, Elisha, and Joseph were walking alongside the one whom God called to be their mentor, it was a position of servanthood. These men were learning firsthand as they observed their teacher, witnessing both successes and failures. Through these seasons of instruction, they had to resolve to be teachable, to accept correction and rebuke, and to refuse to pick up offense. In our generation, we are blessed to live in a time where we can glean from so many different generals of the faith. In order to pull on the anointing in their lives, you need to allow yourself to be connected and submitted to them.

Remember, this isn't limited to Five-Fold ministry. God wants us to walk in our ministry and the mantle He has on our lives! You have a call on your life that is integral to the work that God wants to do while you are here on earth. God will work through the fullness of preparation, leading you to the point where you can cross the threshold and leave your past behind you. If you are willing to go after the mantle God is calling you to, there is a greater anointing than what you can comprehend! Just like Elisha went after Elijah and boldly asked for a double portion, put your own plans aside and seek out what God has for you! God has given you a specific mantle for a specific purpose to the body of Christ. He has positioned you to walk forward in your lane, continuing in your ministry and seeing the suddenlies happening all around. As the body of Christ grasps the concept of working together to accomplish the mandate He has given us, we will see His victory!

"But this one thing I do, forgetting those things which are behind, and reaching forth unto those things which are before, I press toward the mark for the prize of the high calling of God in Christ Jesus. Let us therefore, as many as be perfect, be thus minded: and if in anything ye be otherwise minded, God shall revel even this unto you"

— PHILIPPIANS 3:13-15

CHAPTER 11

CROSS THE THRESHOLD (OUT OF YOUR PAST)

God is calling His people to move forward—out of the shadows, out of the background, and into an active position. It is time for the church to walk in obedience to what the word calls us to, acting as the bride that Christ will return for! This is a monumental stage where we are seeing God move in miraculous ways, seeing signs that can only be explained through the understanding of Kairos' time. These are opportune moments, and I believe that people will finally walk into their destinies as they cross the threshold into their future.

Many believe in God's biblical promises to come to pass, the ability to walk into the "next" that He has for them, and also walking in the fullness of His calling in their lives! We can see in scripture that the way in which you respond to adversity, challenges, or direction from God can affect seeing the door open in your life. We must be aware of God's voice and also other voices that may be vying for our attention. In John 10:7b-10 (MSG), "I'll be explicit, then. I am the gate for the sheep. All those others are up to no good—sheep rustlers, every one of them. But the sheep didn't listen to them. I am the gate. Anyone who goes through me will be cared for and will freely go in and out and find pasture. A thief is only there to steal, kill, and destroy. I came so that they can have real and eternal life, more and better life than they ever dreamed of." We also know from Jeremiah that God has promises of hope and a future for His people; unfortunately, many times, we take our eyes off of our savior and turn to the temporal concerns of our flesh.

In the Old Testament, we can read of God's desire to walk in communion with Adam and Eve. In Genesis 3:1, God had no choice but to change the relationship because of Adam and Eve's actions. They questioned the word God had spoken and listened to an adversary. We also can observe His plan for Moses to help the Israelites escape from Egypt and then deliver them to the Promised Land. Doors were ready to be opened for them to cross the threshold; however, due to their responses, fear, and lack of faith, the majority of them never saw their promise come to fruition! Caleb and Joshua had been willing to walk forward with faith, declaring the faithfulness of God; they were the only two who would cross the threshold and experience that open door. The result may have been very different for the Israelites had they considered all of the ways in which God had provided.

DOORS TO THE THRESHOLD

In previous chapters, we have mentioned God opening doors, but also our tendency to either open doors ourselves or allow doors to remain open even though God has told us to move on. Some of those doors are keeping us from crossing over the threshold and taking hold of our miracles and the promises that we believe in! You have a personal responsibility to make the effort to cross that threshold. God is calling us to walk into that next room, that next level. It is vitally important to consider how you react in bad situations. Personally, I believe that some doors have remained closed for me in certain areas because I have not reacted correctly. This is exactly what happened with the Israelites as well! The time is now. You must identify how to cross the threshold into your next because God has great things prepared for you on the other side of this door.

We have looked at this passage previously, describing when Paul and Silas were in prison and then were miraculously freed. I now want to view it from a different perspective. Acts 16:25-34 shows us the correct way to react when there is trouble and also how God can be glorified through those situations. It was around midnight, which was the darkest point of the day. Paul and Silas were praying and singing hymns to God. And the other prisoners were listening. Suddenly, there was a massive earthquake, and the prison was shaken to its foundation. All the doors immediately flew open, and the chains of every prisoner fell off. The jailer woke up to see the prison doors wide open. He assumed the prisoners had escaped, so he drew his sword to kill himself. Paul then shouted to him, saying, "Stop, don't kill yourself. We are all here." (v. 28)

"The jailer called for lights, ran to the dungeon, fell down, trembling before Paul and Silas. Then he brought them out and asked sirs, what must I do to be saved?" (v.29, 30) The message of the gospel had not been preached. It had been lived. They replied, believe in the Lord Jesus. They shared the word of the Lord with him and with all who lived in his household. Even at that hour of the night, the jailer cared for them and washed their wounds. Then, he and everyone in his house were immediately baptized. He brought them into the house and set a mill before them. And he and his entire household rejoiced because they all believed in God. (v. 31-34)

FOCUS ON YOUR CONVERSATION

What are you currently doing when you are in shackles and behind locked doors? You may not be where you want to be yet, but what you do in your current situation can be the key to allowing you to move forward. You may be finding that you have not crossed the threshold or walked through the open door that God has for you. You may even be thinking that the door has yet to be opened for you. The first thing that I see these men of God doing, is that they begin to focus on their conversation with God. Paul and Silas were in jail with shackles on, behind literally closed doors, and yet they were not disturbed or distracted from what God was saying about their life. Regardless of what is going on around you, you need to focus on your conversation with God. What are you and God talking about right now? When I hear God's voice, I'm obedient to do what God said, and I trust him. Your conversation or your prayer life is the key that's going to unlock what's next in your life. When you have the right outlook on your situation, or your problem is being held in the correct perspective compared to your source, you are able to pray appropriately. At that point, the earth will move. God will bust up the foundations of every prison that has held you captive in your life. He will break the shackles for you.

KEEP YOUR PRAISE ON

We can also see from scripture that Paul and Silas were singing hymns to the Lord. They were singing songs celebrating the faithful God they serve! When you are facing an obstacle, you need to keep your praise and your joy. God was listening. He was listening for the sound of faith. He was listening for joy. He was listening for praise. He was listening for worship. I imagine that Paul and Silas would have been acting very differently if they had been allowing their flesh to rule. They could have been focusing on the smell, the pain, their hunger, and fear. The outcome would have shifted if they had talked about the shackles, blisters, and how cold or bad it was. They didn't wait to pray or sing praises until their flesh felt like it. Regardless of your situation, don't wait until you feel like it. In order for faith to begin to operate, you're going to have to praise him on this side of the threshold. It is amazing how quickly your spirit strengthens as you focus on praising and worshipping your savior! If you are waiting to see something specific, manifest in your life, standing on faith is not waiting until He brings it to pass to thank Him for it! Faith is thanking Him for it now! Declaring with your words that you have received the promise and believe that it will soon manifest in the natural!

BRING HIM INTO FOCUS

Whatever gets the majority of your words is what is reigning in your heart. If your speech is primarily focused on your problems, the problems end up becoming your Lord. If you always talk about your situation, focusing on how bad it is, then you should expect to stay there. At any moment, they could have changed their conversation, and that place would've become their Lord. Now that outlook is reigning and ruling in your life. Maybe for you, it is your sickness, finances, or relationships. The "problem" itself is irrelevant to how you are able to get through it. Instead of allowing themselves to be caught up in the moment, they were caught up in Him, and they said, "You rule in reign in my life, so our words are going to glorify you."

They praised God while in prison, even though they'd been beaten, thrown into prison, and remained shackled. They sang hymns and prayed. They praised in such a bad situation that it caused those around them to take notice and listen to them. How you act under pressure will determine how much attention people pay to your life. If you claim to have faith, is your lifestyle demonstrating it? People are watching you. Your praise, your worship, and your prayer will help not only you but also the people around you. When conflict comes up in your life, you remain unshakable. Your foundation is on the rock, not on sinking sand, and you don't falter. That testimony speaks volumes to those who are around you. When Paul testifies that he is content in all things—whether he had much or little, he had joy. Never lose sight of the fact that what you are doing can shake the world around you.

Sometimes, what you don't do is more important than you think. Roman law required jailers to take personal responsibility for prisoners. That's why that jailer was going to fall on his sword because it was his fault no matter what. So Paul, Silas, and the other prisoners didn't leave when their chains came off; if they had, the jailer would have been put to death or killed himself. This is why he placed them into the inner prison and fastened their feet in stalks. They took on personal responsibility for everybody else around them, even the people who held them captive. They never stepped out of love for that jailer. The very one who beat them on the way to jail was the one cleaning their wounds on the way out of jail.

A STRONGER FLOW

Essentially, Paul and Silas were faced with what many would consider a serious or life-altering situation. Even with high stakes, they resisted the temptation to focus on the obstacles and kept their eyes on God; they were an example to the people around them. There is a vision the Holy Spirit gave me that helped me understand the importance of this attitude. Holy Spirit showed me a river. When a river first begins to flow, it has obstacles. What does it do? It doesn't slow down and talk to the obstacle. It just sends more flow. So this flow that comes must become stronger and greater to push you out of the rooms you were previously in through new doors, across thresholds, and into new places. Doors are going to bust open because of the flow. Some doors have to be kicked down, and some doors will be flowed down. There will be no barriers or dams. Once you begin to flow in the river, the river ends up dictating its direction. A river is not determined by the course that it flows in; sometimes, it will modify the borders of what is around it! God can move you in situations and in the flow of your life as long as you are focused on flowing with the river!

You may also look at this from the perspective of having walked in a measure of the Holy Spirit but experiencing a struggle or warfare. God is saying, don't worry; I will stand with you there. I believe that this river can get deeper and wider and stronger and fiercer than it ever has been in your life. I believe that in this next season when we open up our mouths, and the power comes, we will witness a move of God. The power of God will be cast on situations, and the result is for people to experience miracles, signs, and wonders. The world is waiting on us to rise up with this river, this flow of the spirit of God that's flowing out of our life. God is calling His church to step into the greater.

BREAK THE LOCKS

God has great things prepared for you, just like the strong flow in the river. The obstacles you keep running into could be similar to a lock on a door that you're trying to go through. He will show you if there are behaviors that you need to change in your life or things you need to let go of from your past, which will result in you being able to walk across that threshold as soon as the locks break free. This isn't something to hesitate on or procrastinate and put off until tomorrow. If something is holding you back, you need to examine your life, your relationship with God, and the things He has told you to do. The key to unlocking those doors is to let go of your past, putting away any dreams that have been delayed. Once you have stopped living in the past, you have to start moving forward! That's where the prize is, and that's where true peace and victory are found. Unbelief looks at the past and says, "See, it can't be done." But faith steps out, knowing that the victory has already been won. Close the doors to the lies that the devil tries to convince you of and claim the promises of God!

If you take God at His Word, you can wake up every morning to a fresh start. You can live a life free from the past. You can do this! Replace thoughts of yesterday's problems and failures with God's word about your future. As you do that, hope will start replacing disappointment and depression. God is going to show up in your present and prophesy about your future, which will suddenly become your past. Get ready to step across the threshold into what God has for your future. Don't be afraid, and don't be held back. God has something great for you beyond the open door.

"But this one thing I do, forgetting those things which are behind, and reaching forth unto those things which are before, I press toward the mark for the prize of the high calling of God in Christ Jesus. Let us therefore, as many as be perfect, be thus minded: and if in anything ye be otherwise minded, God shall revel even this unto you" (Philippians 3:13-15)

COMPLETING THE PUZZLE

There are choices we make as we accomplish the tasks that are scheduled for each day. How could it be manageable, or better yet a focus, to shift priority to the people around us as we go about our day? In our fast-moving society, it is a tendency to set a goal of completing a grocery trip or school pickup line as quickly as possible and interacting with as few people as possible. While that may check the box in the responsibilities we have given ourselves, how does that answer the mandate we are to be a part of? Holy Spirit desires to go with you on a "treasure hunt," seeking His children whose lives could be changed if someone was willing to listen, smile, or pray! As you make yourself available for His use, He will not only lead you but also give you the words and tools to carry out The Great Commission!

God will continue to develop your character and traits through your relationship with Himself and others. I encourage you to pray about the people in your life, with whom you have close relationships, and with whom there is vulnerability. I encourage asking God if any of those people are in your life for a relationship similar to Moses and Joshua, whether you are in a position to speak into their life or you are in a season to be gleaned from what they have to teach. In addition to personal relationships, there may also be ministries of people that you connect with, even on the national level, that support the development of your character. Asking for God to show you ministries you can move alongside or those that move in a particular flow can be instrumental in how you are growing and preparing for the mantle He has.

As you are navigating the pruning of preparation for the mantle He is calling you to, or feeling like you're running on a treadmill toward your goal and just not getting anywhere, it is essential to remember that as we are following

His leading, He has a plan and purpose for everything He does. As we walk in His preparation, He is working all things together! His preparation allows us to carry the mantle for His Kingdom more effectively and be a light to the people around us! Don't allow outsiders to cast doubt at what you know to be God working out the fullness of preparation in your life. God is working through time of preparation: teaching, pruning, and watering for the fullness of time when the sprout suddenly appears from the ground!

As we are faithful and obedient to what God calls us to do, we know He will be faithful in His promises. It is easy to get caught up in Chronos' time of it all, getting stuck on whether or not it is possible. Matthew 19:26 (MSG) says, "Jesus looked hard at them and said, 'No chance at all if you think you can pull it off yourself. Every chance in the world if you trust God to do it.'" The promises you believe in become simple when considering how limitless our God is. He is not held back by complexity or time and can make things happen overnight and instantaneously! The widow with Elisha may have believed she would never receive a breakthrough, but her miracle arrived just in time. As we continue to press forward in our relationship with our savior, we can know with confidence that He can change our situation suddenly! God can be trusted. If He has spoken it, He has the ability to perform it, and He is faithful.

Just like Esther, you were created for such a time as this. The world around you needs you to step into what God called you to do. God planned for you to be where you are in the time you are living in. He has wonderful plans for you: for the things He desires to come to pass in your life and assignments for you to accomplish within the mantle He has called you to. He neither called nor intended for his children to stand silently as people continue to be lost and hurting in our world. Matthew 5:14-16 (NASB 2020) says, "You are the light of the world. A city set on a hill cannot be hidden, nor do people light a lamp and put it under a basket, but on the lampstand, and it gives light to all who are in the house. Your light must shine before people so they may see your good works, and glorify your father who is in heaven."

As believers establish the foundation of who they are in Christ and the call that is on their lives, I believe we will see more and more believers grasp the call to action: waking up from their slumber, realizing the state of our nation, and then (and only then) our voice will once again be heard. Just like Moses, it's time to rise and be an example for the people. Let us shout with the passion of the Israelites in Joshua 6:1, which brought the walls of Jericho tumbling to the ground! Let us take our place to rebuild the wall with Nehemiah and fight for our children and our children's children. We must protect the future generations! The Time is Now!

NOTES

CHAPTER 2

Hagin, K. E. (2010). I Believe in Visions (2nd ed., pp. 46-47). RHEMA Bible Church AKA Kenneth Hagin Ministries, Inc. ISBN 978-1-60616-751-9.

CHAPTER 3

Olive Tree Bible Software, Inc. (2020). Enhanced Strong's Dictionary (Original publication 2011). Olive Tree Bible Software.

Merriam-Webster. (n.d.). Opportunity. In Merriam-Webster.com dictionary. Retrieved March 7, 2024, from https://www.merriam -webster.com/dictionary/opportunity

Merriam-Webster. (n.d.). Courage. In Merriam-Webster.com dictionary. Retrieved March 7, 2024, from https://www.merriam -webster.com/dictionary/courage

Merriam-Webster. (n.d.). Seize. In Merriam-Webster.com dictionary. Retrieved March 7, 2024, from https://www.merriam -webster.com/dictionary/seize.

CHAPTER 4

Olive Tree Bible Software, Inc. (2020). Enhanced Strong's Dictionary (Original publication 2011). Olive Tree Bible Software.

CHAPTER 5

Merriam-Webster. (n.d.). Preparation. In Merriam-Webster.com dictionary. Retrieved March 7, 2024, from https://www.merriam -webster.com/dictionary/preparation

Graham, F. (2018, March 19). A Biblical worldview in today's culture. Billy Graham Evangelistic Association. Retrieved March 8, 2024, from https://www.billygraham.ca/stories/franklin-graham -a-biblical-worldview-in-todays-culture/

Guttmacher Institute. (2024, January 17). Number of abortions in the United States likely to be higher in 2023 than 2020. Retrieved March 8, 2024, from https://www.guttmacher.org/news-release /2024/number-abortions-united-states-likely-be-higher-2023-2020

Newport, F. (2022, July 6). Fewer in U.S. view Bible as literal word of God. Gallup. Retrieved March 8, 2024, from https://news.gallup .com/poll/394262/fewer-bible-literal-word-god.aspx

CHAPTER 8

"Mandate, N." Oxford English Dictionary, Oxford UP, September 2023, https://doi.org/10.1093/OED/1019514310.

Ravenhill, L. (2004). Why revival tarries. Bethany House Publishers.

Barna Group. (2018, March 27). 51% of Churchgoers Don't Know of the Great Commission. Retrieved March 8, 2024, from https://www.barna.com/research/half-churchgoers-not-heard -great-commission/

www.ingramcontent.com/pod-product-compliance
Lightning Source LLC
Chambersburg PA
CBHW051207120626
46547CB00013B/1245